Chili and Chocolate Cake

My Recipe for Staying Anchored In
The Storms of Life

By
Joyce Schneider

Chili and Chocolate Cake, My Recipe for Staying Anchored In the Storms of Life
Copyright © 2011 by Joyce Schneider. All rights reserved.

No part of this publication may be reproduced, stored in a retrieval system or transmitted in any way by any means, electronic, mechanical, photocopy, recording or otherwise without the prior permission of the author except as provided by USA copyright law.

All Scripture references are King James Version, unless otherwise indicated.

Published in the United States of America
ISBN: 978-1545445945
Recovery/Women
17.05.25

To My Bobby -
Our love knows no beginning,
it will see no end–it is infinite.
The path we have traveled has been
rough, but never rocky.
It has allowed us to strengthen and to grow.
Now, as we bond together,
the future holds nothing but promise,
because we are as one.
October 7, 1995

Acknowledgements

Wow, I truly don't know where to start here—there are so many people that I want to thank for their help in bringing this book to fruition. They say it takes a village to raise a child, well I think it takes a village to write and publish a book! So to my own special village, I say a heartfelt, "Thank you!"

To Cindy Hollingsworth, my very special mentor and very good friend, who spent so much time with me, holding me when I cried and jumping up and down with me when I rejoiced, but always encouraging me to take that next step towards Jesus. And who never stopped saying, "Write it down, Joyce." You are such an encouragement to me, my friend, and to you I give my eternal thanks!

To all my Bible girls, who walked with me through my journey, always praying for me and for this book—you know who you are. I couldn't have done it without you. I love each and every one of you; you are very special to me.

To Vicki Gardner, my business partner and my very special friend—your encouragement meant everything to me. Thank you for believing in me.

To my aunt, Nancy Kearns, and my friend, Beverly DeLozier, who helped me figure out the grammar part of how a book is supposed to come together. I know they won't believe it, but I really did get A's on my term papers. Thank you both for struggling through the p's and q's of this production.

To my parents, Gerald and Carolyn Prouty, thank you for enduring and loving me during all those years that I know all of us would just as soon forget. Thank you for allowing me to drag them back out. And thank you for teaching me to never quit. I love you both.

To my grandmother, Betty Lyons, who never stopped praying for me. You have a special place in my heart. I'm so sorry you've had to endure such a tough year. God's blessings to you.

To my sons, Carson and Chase Schneider—you truly did give me the inspiration to never give up. I love you both so very much. You are two very special little boys.

To my Bobby, who is the world's greatest husband and father, and who has never stopped loving me, in spite of myself. And who was so willing to allow me to reveal our personal lives to the world. You are one-of-a-kind. I love you forever.

But most of all, I thank You, Lord Jesus, for giving me the life that enabled me to go on this journey, for giving me the ability to put all of my thoughts into words, and for putting all the broken pieces back together and turning me into a vessel that Your light could shine through. I love you with all my heart and with all my soul.

Table of Contents

What Does Chili Have To Do With God? 11
Set Free! 15
A Life Decision 23
Pride Comes Before A Fall 37
Through The Fire 43
My Golden Child 57
The Journey Back 67
Where To Go Now? 79
Gain Through The Pain 83
Being Real 93
Being Humbled 105
Modern Day Miracle 111
Wrestling With The Enemy 121
Find Your Purpose 135
Winning The Battle 143
A Child's Heart 149
Moving Forward 157
Enough 161
Joyce's Chili Recipe 171
Notes 173
The End...For Now 175

What Does Chili Have To Do With God?

When I told one of my friends the title I was thinking of for my book, she laughed and said, "People may think it's a cookbook."

So I want to start off by saying, this is *not* a cookbook, although I will most definitely give you my recipe for chili. The chocolate cake I can't claim fame to; Betty Crocker gets that.

Chili and chocolate cake represent *stability* in my life during a time when nothing was stable...a time when I was being tossed around, as my husband said to me one night, "...like a ship in an ocean."

That's not exactly how you want your husband to describe you, but he was 100% correct, and unfortunately at the time, I had no clue as to how to calm the seas that were surrounding me and threatening to capsize me as each new wave came crashing over my life.

Where to start? That is the big question. There are so many beginnings, so many endings, and so many places I'm still in the middle of...

Chili and Chocolate Cake

> "Gratitude. More aware of what you have than what you don't. Recognizing the treasure in the simple—a child's hug, fertile soil, a golden sunset. Relishing in the comfort of the common—a warm bed, a hot meal, a clean shirt."
> —Max Lucado [1]

Be anxious for nothing, but in everything by prayer and supplication, with thanksgiving, let your requests be made known to God; and the peace of God, which surpasses all understanding, will guard your hearts and minds through Christ Jesus.
Philippians 4:6, 7 (NKJV)

You are going to get to know me quite well by the time you finish this story, but let me start you off with a little background information. I am forty-four years old, and I live in southwest Florida, with my wonderful husband of nine years, Bobby, and my two sons, Carson, seven, and Chase, who is five.

I'm just a regular person; a wife, a mother, a friend.

> "I am only a small container of Your Spirit, Lord. Let others be affected by the spill-over."
> —Neva Coyle [2]

I volunteer each week for my son's first grade class at school, teach Sunday School to a group of rambunctious two- and three-year-olds, lead a weekly mom-based woman's Bible study, and do a hundred other activities that fill my day. I am probably a lot like you.

I grew up in a Christian home in southeast Ohio with a loving family and I went to church all my life. Unfortunately I never knew what it meant to have a personal relationship with Jesus Christ. I heard lots of people talk about it, but I just never could figure out what the *big deal* was.

I would hear testimony after testimony of what God had done for others, and as much as I wanted to know Him, for whatever reason, I just didn't know how to let Him into my life. Part of me was extremely fearful of a God who could hurl lightning bolts and strike men down dead, but another part of me was rebellious and a huge know-it-all, someone who didn't *need* God. Someone who thought she could take care of herself.

Now, I had prayed the prayer of salvation when I was young, probably at the age of about eight or nine, but I still never felt like Jesus was really a part of my life. I would pray and pray, but never felt like He ever answered me, or even heard me for that matter.

I'll get to more of that part of the story a bit later, but for now, the best place to start is in the middle.

(We'll work through the beginnings and the endings together as we go.)

> "When we confine our relationship with God to only the accumulation of information about him, we may miss the experience of his presence or fail to realize that the act of adoring God is very different from merely reading about adoring him."
> —Brenda Waggoner, Fairy Tale Faith [3]

My little children, let us not love in word or in tongue, but in deed and in truth. And by this we know that we are of the truth, and shall assure our hearts before Him. For if our heart condemns us, God is greater than our heart, and knows all things.

I John 3:18–20 (NKJV)

Set Free!

Every Thursday night, our family goes to the weekly potluck supper at our church. It's a time to simply relax, enjoy dinner, and fellowship with one another. On one Thursday night in July of 2002, one of my friends asked me if everything was okay. I assured her it was and that I was fine. As I was saying goodbye to another friend, she asked me the same question, and I gave her the same answer. On my way home I started pondering the question myself. *Was I really fine?* The next day I sent my friend an e-mail thanking her for her concern and started sharing with her what I felt was actually bothering me.

I had experienced a miscarriage (my second) in August of 2000, and I'd never really been able to get over losing the baby and my ache for another child. I tried to give it to the Lord, but in doing so, I thought I had to act like I no longer cared about having a baby, and as much as I tried, it just didn't work for me. It was a lie, and everyone knows you can't lie to God. By trying to act like I no longer cared about having a baby I was making myself more and more miserable! The whole while I was trying to sort it all out, I realized

Chili and Chocolate Cake

I was carrying a heavy burden that was only getting worse!

After admitting my problem to my friend, she suggested we get together for an evening of prayer, and see if God would reveal to me anything that I needed to deal with, so that healing from this burden could begin. I was so miserable that I agreed to go, although I was really not comfortable discussing the issue. I didn't even talk to my husband about babies. (I have a terrible tendency to push everything down inside me as a way of trying to forget it all. Unfortunately, that tactic was not working this time.)

I met with my friend, and we just sat in her living room and started praying, asking God to reveal, whatever needed to be dealt with. And the Lord, being the awesome Creator that He is, started revealing to me, with incredible clarity, why I was so miserable. It was truly awesome! He took me all over my life and back again, and finally, the truth was revealed!

Let me at this point explain a little about my past. My young adult days were not pleasing to the Lord. Even though I had professed to be a Christian as a child, I had never actually experienced a personal relationship with Jesus Christ. As I told you earlier, I just couldn't figure out what the *big deal* about Jesus was. I lived a life that now causes me to literally cringe in pain.

Pleasing the *Lord* was last on my list of priorities, and pleasing *me* was first! And, I did please myself in every way known to man, with no holds barred...I abused alcohol, drugs, men...there were no limits!

I mellowed out a bit when, at the age of 31, I met the man who was to become my husband. We married, after a few years of living together, and set out to start a family. On the outside I was pretty much the perfect wife and mother, but I still had not known the Lord in an intimate, personal way. Then, after my second miscarriage, I became physically and mentally depleted. I hit as low as I could go, and then I started searching for a way out of my abyss. At that time, the Lord graciously reached down His hand and pulled me out of that blackness. I realized that I did not truly know him and I finally accepted Him as my Lord and Savior. For the first time in my life, I started to understand what the *big deal* was. I could not get enough of Him! I was ready to make up for lost time!

I spent the next couple of years learning God's Word and studying as much about Jesus as possible, pushing the pain of my miscarriages down to the depths of my soul, where all the bad stuff had always been pushed before. I knew, from my personal studies, that I had to give this thing to God, so I did...or at least I tried. But as I said earlier, I thought giving it to God meant not desiring another child and that was far from the truth.

In reality, I still kept track of the days in my cycle

that were best for conception. Waves of disappointment would rush over me each month when my period came. I could not hide the pain.

I didn't understand; I knew the Lord, He was my Savior, and I had even asked Him to take my burden from me, so why was I on a continuous emotional roller coaster consumed with the idea of having another baby to the degree that I could not touch a newborn baby or even get close enough to look one in the face? The pain was just too deep.

That was my burden as I came to the Lord that evening at my friend's home, not sure where it would go, but desperate for my pain to end. Even a slow ebb would be better than the constant ache in my heart.

And our wonderful Lord, in a way that only He could accomplish, began a healing process in me that very night. He cleansed me of the junk that I had been carrying around inside of me for years and years! It was awesome! I went from feeling like I was the scum of the earth to feeling like I was *His chosen vessel!*

I had listened to the enemy tell me over and over again, that I was bad, and unforgivable, and I had lived with that shame and guilt for so many years. That evening, the Lord told me I was *His* and I was *white as snow!*

You see, part of my pain was due to the fact that I had had an abortion many years earlier. I was alone and unmarried with no money and nowhere to turn (my wrong belief structure). I believed, at that time, my only recourse was to have an abortion. The guilt and shame of that event had haunted me every day of my life since. I'll tell you a bit more about this situation further down the road.

When I came to know the Lord, I had repented of my past, I thought, but I had actually never allowed *myself* to forgive *me* for all the sins I had committed. God forgave me, but I had never forgiven *myself.* God gave me the power of forgiveness that evening, and what freedom came over me, freedom like I haven't had in years!! Actual weights just lifted off my heart and my soul! I was truly bouncing off the walls!

That night God gave me this verse:

Come near to God and He will come near to you...
James 4:8 (NIV)

Wow...how true!

God so much wants us near Him! Just as we love our children and want nothing more than to hang out with them, our Heavenly Father longs for us to just hang out with Him. He wants us to simply draw near to Him! But we have to take that first step!

I spent the next week simply basking in my new-found freedom. I felt like I was literally bouncing off the walls! I was so excited to finally be free from that heavy burden I had been dragging around for so long.

I went back to visit my friend a second time, the next week, and we prayed again. Just as a check up, so to speak, to see if there was anything else that needed to come out. As it turned out, the Lord was not finished with me yet. He revealed more things from my past that I had never dealt with. God showed me that He wanted me to let go of my *entire* past and to forgive myself from all the things I had done.

He had already forgiven me the night He died on the cross. It was my turn now to forgive myself and to let all of that past sin go. It took a lot of effort for me to dredge up those past experiences, and I really didn't get a sense of release while praying. But later that evening, after returning home, past memories that had been forgotten and buried deep inside myself, came alive once again. Memories for which I needed to repent, be forgiven, and move on. It was a most painful process to revisit those days, but the peace and comfort that followed was incredible!

God left me with this thought: **believe and receive.** When I looked it up in the scriptures, I found the following:

The Apostle Paul is writing to Timothy:

Here is a trustworthy saying that deserves full acceptance: Christ Jesus came into the world to save sinners—of whom I am the worst. But for that very reason I was shown mercy so that in me, the worst of

sinners, Christ Jesus might display his unlimited patience as an example for those who would believe on him and receive eternal life.
1 Timothy 1:15–16 (NIV)

There was my **believe and receive!** I felt like I was the worst of sinners, yet Jesus Christ died for me, so that I could *believe* in Him and *receive* eternal life. Jesus didn't care about my past; He only cared about my present and what my future could be, with Him.

Once I discovered this newfound freedom from the guilt and shame of my past, God decided I was ready for a ministry! Yes, me, the person who had spent so many years not following God and living a life of sin, was now at a point in my life where God could use me to help someone else. God revealed to me that I needed to go and talk to others about my past, the consequences of my sin, and what it could mean to be set free from the burdens and guilt of a past life.

Although I realized that I made my own wrong choices all those years ago, I still felt like if it hadn't been so easy for me to do so that I may have made different choices. If someone would have looked me in the face and made me aware of my consequences or if someone had held me accountable for my actions, I might not have taken the road I did.

I know I cannot undo my past, but I have finally forgiven myself, and know now that God wants me to share my story with others in the hope that maybe something I say will touch another.

God is so good! For years, I couldn't even say the word *abortion* and today I can tell my story to strangers, without even the slightest hesitancy or without the guilt that has riddled me for so long. It is my prayer that my story might make a difference somehow, to someone.

> "We can do no great things, only small things with great love."
> —Mother Teresa

And these words which I command you today shall be in your heart. You shall teach them diligently to your children, and shall talk of them when you sit in your house, when you walk by the way, when you lie down, and when you rise up. You shall bind them as a sign on your hand, and they shall be as frontlets between your eyes. You shall write them on the doorposts of your house and on your gates.

Deuteronomy 6:6–9 (NKJV)

Your testimonies also are my delight, and my counselors.

Psalm 119:24 (NKJV)

A Life Decision

I'd like to share in a little more detail with you how I ended up making the decision to have an abortion. I just didn't wake up one day and decide, out of the blue, to kill my baby. This decision came about as a result of years of not making the right choices.

I'm not going to go into Biblical teachings on abortion, nor am I going to go into medical terminology or legal issues. What I want to explain to you is *how this one simple word can **ruin** your entire life,* and **why** I know this to be true.

As I stated earlier, I grew up in a Christian home with three sisters, a brother, and both of my parents. We went to church every Sunday, and although I had asked Jesus into my heart when I was about eight or nine, I never felt like I had a personal relationship with the Lord. I just didn't get what the big deal was with God.

I was actually very afraid of God. I had made him out to be very strict and judgmental, in my mind, and I just couldn't get past those preconceptions. My parents took us to church, but we didn't spend much time discussing God or Jesus at home, so my perception of God was the wrong thoughts that were swimming around in my brain. I knew right from wrong—don't get me wrong—my parents were quite strict with me, but most times I made the choices that I wanted, not what God wanted for me.

When I was fifteen, a couple of my friends decided that it was time for me to get a taste of alcohol. I had never done drugs or drank, up to this point, but they kept telling me how much fun it was, so I decided to give it a shot. The next Friday night, instead of going to the sock hop at school, my friends and I picked up a six pack of beer and a couple of bottles of cheap wine and we drove around town and proceeded to get smashed.

That first night of *fun* resulted in me throwing up all over myself, the girl driving the car hitting a mailbox with her dad's car, and another friend going a little crazy and running around uncontrollably like a wild person out in a field. On top of this was the fact that I had lied to my parents about my activities. That night marked the beginning of years of destructive choices in my life.

I continued on my destructive path with smoking my first joint and experimenting with quite a few other drugs. Drinking and doing drugs became a major part of my life; all done in secret and all without my parent's knowledge.

I became very adept at lying and at being sick on the sly. Alcohol is a poison, and when you put poison into your body, it makes you sick! That is something your friends forget to tell you when they hand you that first drink—how terrible you are going to feel the next day!

One morning I thought it would be cool to take a drug called "PCP" before school. I popped it on the school bus, on my way to school. By second period, I had turned into a zombie. Unfortunately, I had forgotten that we were going to have an Algebra test that morning. I was so messed up, that I could only write my name on the paper and turn it back in. My teacher was a little confused as to why I couldn't take the test since I was typically close to a straight-A student. But I simply told him I was sick and not feeling too well, and he let it go, since I had never done anything like that before in his class.

My high school years continued on in this manner, skipping classes to go out and get high, leaving games to drink, anytime I was around my friends, was an excuse to party.

When I went away to college, my roommate came to school with a quarter pound bag of pot in her backpack and a bottle full of all sorts of pills! Thus began two years of constant drugging and drinking. In high school I always had to hide my activities from my parents, but now that I lived in my own house, I was free to do as I wished. And that is just what I did...again making choices that took me down a road that Jesus would not have chosen for me.

I began sleeping around with guys, because my roommate assured me that it was a cool thing to do. I didn't want to be a nerdy virgin. Up to that point in time, I had never really spent much time with guys—I just enjoyed hanging out with my buddies. But my roommate convinced me that sex was the ticket, and I let her fix me up with her friends. Sex became just another activity to add to our recreational habits. Because I let the peer pressure influence me, I allowed her to talk me into going on the pill, with no thought to the consequences of that decision or how it might affect me later on in my life.

I moved to Naples when I was 21. A few months later I met a guy at the beach and started my first venture into living together with my boyfriend, his four roommates, and myself! Wow, talk about romantic! But I was young and in the party mode, and with our lifestyle there was always someone around eager to share a buzz with!

We all ended up moving to Daytona Beach together. We told our parents it was to continue on in college, but most of the time we were too busy partying to make it to school. We quit after the first two semesters and took jobs in restaurants. Daytona Beach was a crazy place to live and it fit right into our lifestyle!

After a couple of years, my boyfriend and I split

up, and I moved back to Naples. I was pretty devastated because I had believed that we would get married and have a family, which was really what my heart desired at that point. Even in the midst of all the parties, I still knew I wanted to settle down and start a family. But he was too young and too wild to even consider settling down. Because we had never made that commitment to get married, there was nothing binding to keep us together when the struggles came.

He did follow me back to Naples shortly thereafter. He would pop in on occasion for a night together; we were still *buddies* you see. But, most of the time, he was busy pursuing a rich, older woman. One weekend, he showed up and stayed with me for three days. I had run out of my birth control pills the month before, and simply forgot to refill my prescription. I wasn't very clear-headed back then as I was always either hungover or buzzed, so forgetting my pills was a common occurrence.

Six weeks later, however, when my period was late, I realized the consequence of my decisions was going to be a little more serious: I discovered that I was pregnant. I had very little money, no husband, no boyfriend (he was back with his wealthy divorcée by then), and no thought of how I could be a mother to a baby.

I was devastated. I couldn't have a baby! I couldn't tell my parents I was pregnant! I was even so naïve that I felt I couldn't tell anyone I was pregnant. Today, I know all those fears could have been overcome, and overcome very easily, but as I said before, I was not thinking clearly. Too many beers and too many joints had left me with a mind that just didn't process information clearly.

In my mind, I felt like I had no one to turn to for help. I was ashamed that I was pregnant and didn't even have a boyfriend! I decided that having an abortion was my only option. So, I made the appointment and I went to the clinic that morning and allowed my baby to be killed.

I can still remember that day, clear as a bell. I really didn't even want to go through with it by that point. (I had found out I was pregnant a few weeks before Christmas but was told they couldn't do the abortion till after the New Year.) In the meantime, I was actually starting to accept the fact that I was carrying a baby inside of me. Unfortunately, since I had already made my decision to have the abortion, I felt like there was no turning back. No one told me that the consequences of that decision would haunt me for the rest of my life.

No one told me that I was going to kill a real, live, little baby inside of me. Do you know that at 10 weeks, a baby has all of the vital organs to survive? It is just a miniature little person. At 24 weeks, a baby can actually survive outside the womb.

I didn't know any of these things and I didn't want to know them. I didn't want to know what they were going to do or how they were going to do it. I just wanted to be *unpregnant* so that I could go on with my life. I was only thinking of myself at that point.

Having that abortion started me on a life of total despair. If I drank before, I drank twice as much after. If I did drugs before, I did twice as many after. If I slept with guys before, I slept with more after. Anything I could do to numb myself from what I had done, I did. I lived in a constant state of numbness and depression.

I actually decided one night that I might just as well kill myself, as I had nothing to live for. I hated my life of drugs, alcohol, and sex. All I wanted was to be a wife and a mommy, but obviously I wasn't fit for that, I'd already killed my baby, so I might just as well end it for myself.

As I had decided on suicide, I called a good friend to say goodbye, and thank goodness, I did call her! She came over and spent the night with me and helped me to find some reason to live, as this was *definitely* not a good choice either.

I spent the next few years drowning myself in this destructive lifestyle...always ready for the next party. Working and partying were my life. There was no room for anything good, including Jesus Christ.

Then one day, I met a really different guy, Bobby. He wasn't like the rest of the men I knew. Oh sure, he liked to have a beer or two every now and then, but he was quiet and reserved. Something about him told me that he was the man I could start a real life with. I felt he was a man who I could trust.

We lived together for four years and finally decided it was time to get married. I never told Bobby about the abortion, but he knew I had a very wild past. He accepted me for the person he saw inside of me... not the wild Joyce, but the Joyce who constantly talked of being a wife and a mother. He knew I wanted a baby desperately, but he wasn't really sure why it was so important to me. He didn't know the pain that grew inside of me on a daily basis.

About a month into our engagement, I found out I was pregnant. We immediately moved the wedding day up and started making plans to start our family. But, just four weeks into my pregnancy, I lost the baby. My heart was broken. I wanted this little baby. Having a baby had been on my mind for so long, it was all I could think about. And suddenly, I'd lost my baby again!!

Was it my fault, due to the abortion? The guilt flooded me intensely.

After we married, we started trying again to get pregnant. This time we got our first little angel, Carson Robert, followed twenty months later by our second angel, Chase Joseph. I was on top of the world! I had two beautiful little boys, and life was wonderful!

I had changed my lifestyle when I married Bobby. Drinking and drugs were a fading memory of a past life. I was a wife and a mom and life was great. But, there was still something missing. I wasn't sure what it was, but I just didn't feel complete. I still could not stop thinking about that little baby that I had killed so many years before.

Would he have looked like Carson or like Chase? How old would he have been? What would we be doing with him? My heart constantly ached for that little baby, day in and day out.

We started attending a church because we felt like it would be a good thing to do for the boys. Both Bobby and I had grown up in church (not that we were living lives evident of the fact at the time) but we wanted the boys to get that foundation. I fell in love with the praise and worship music at this new church. The church I had grown up in had never had music of this variety before. It reminded me a bit of the contemporary music that I played night and day, but instead of love songs to men or women, they were love songs to God. I just thought that was the neatest thing. I also enjoyed the sermons that the pastor preached. They were straightforward and to the point. In addition to the wonderful music and the great preaching, we had found a nice church family as well. I had never felt like I belonged to the church that I grew up in, so this was a nice change for me...to actually feel like a part of a family again. My own family was not living in our town, so it was extra special to have a close relationship with my friends from church.

Life appeared to be good, on the surface, but inside I was still struggling. I was starting to realize that maybe I didn't have a personal relationship with Jesus. But I still didn't understand what the *big deal* was or how to actually get it.

I went to church every Sunday. I sang praises to the Lord; I even started attending a Bible study, yet that special relationship with Jesus was still eluding me. I would hear the others talking and knew that something was missing there for me. But again, my pride kept me from opening up and sharing my doubts. What would my new friends think if I told them I didn't know if I had a relationship with the Lord or not? That I didn't think I knew the Jesus they knew?

Then, I experienced my second miscarriage in the summer of 2000, and my wonderful, perfect little world did a complete flip-flop. I truly wanted another little angel to add to our nest and my heart was again broken.

This time, I didn't **just** have a miscarriage, I felt as though I had lost one of my babies—like I had lost Carson or Chase. I had already named him and had a picture in my mind of my three little blond-haired, blue-eyed angels!

At the time of this second miscarriage the memories of the abortion came flooding back full force and this time, I could not pull myself out of my despair. I was searching for answers and I soon found out that the only one who had them was Jesus!!

At that point I had three babies up in heaven and I knew I had to find out for certain how I was going to be sure to get there to be with them! I had prayed a prayer to ask Jesus into my heart as a child, as I mentioned earlier, but the life I had led since then was anything but that of a *Christian!*

I needed concrete, solid answers about heaven and my salvation and I got them...*from the Lord!*

WOW...how cool is that?

I finally came to terms with the fact that I didn't have a personal relationship with Jesus and I wanted one, desperately. I asked Jesus to be my Savior and my Lord. I asked for His forgiveness for my sins, and I finally started to understand what it really meant to know Him personally!

For the first time in my entire life I knew, for sure, that when I died, I would go to heaven to be with my Savior and with all my babies! Thank you, Jesus!

And, the best part?...Jesus not only gave me eternal life, but He also forgave me of all my sins, *including* the abortion!

Unfortunately, I did not allow *myself* to forgive me. I spent another couple of years, floundering in a sea of despair. Here I was a follower of Christ, a wife, a mother with two beautiful little boys, and I still was not happy. I still suffered greatly from the guilt and shame of my past and especially from the abortion.

God had forgiven me, but I had never forgiven myself. When this realization finally came through to me, the Lord gently led me to a place, through much prayer and repentance, where I could finally release the bondage of this past sin and be set free!

Through the power of prayer, repentance, and forgiveness, for the first time in almost twenty years I am now free of shame. I can now say the word *abortion* without any guilt or pain.

> *Therefore, if anyone is in Christ, he is a new creation; the old has gone, the new has come!*
> *2 Corinthians 5:17 (NIV)*

Jesus doesn't see the *old me*...all He sees is the *new creature* that I have become!

Thank You, Jesus!

As part of my healing process, Jesus has shown me that I need to share my experiences with others. I need to talk to the youth of today and explain to them how certain choices will affect their lives, and how they can eliminate a lot of pain and grief from their future by making the right life decisions! I also want to help and encourage people who have made bad choices in their past, to see that there is a Savior, who loves them, who will forgive them, and who will bring peace into their lives.

It's all about the choices we make!!

Lord, You tell me that You have hidden Your Word in my heart. Help Your Word to spread from my heart to my words and actions. When people look at me, let them see You. Let them see the evidence of Your Word in my life.

I love you Jesus.

In Your name I pray,
Amen

Your word is a lamp to my feet and a light to my path.
Psalm 119:105 (NKJV)

Your word I have hidden in my heart, that I might not sin against You.
Psalm 119:11 (NKJV)

I will instruct you and teach you in the way you should go; I will guide you with My eye.
Psalm 32:8 (NKJV)

Pride Comes Before A Fall

And so, my life was progressing, yet, I still had a desperate desire for another baby. About a month after receiving my newfound freedom in Christ, during one of our ladies Bible studies, I happened to sit beside a new mom and her beautiful little baby boy, who was about three or four months old.

I had gone ahead and sat down beside them because I had come in late and that was the only seat left in the room. I wasn't worried though because I figured I was healed of all my pain and that it was safe for me to sit there, however, I had no sooner sat down and looked at that little guy when Wham! The pain came flooding back as I stared down into that beautiful little face. It reminded me so much of the two beautiful little faces that God had given me. My stomach lurched, my heart ached, and I wanted to run out. But I stayed and endured the pain.

The next day I realized that it was not right for me to still feel that pain. I mentioned it to my friend, who had been working with me through all the issues, and she was in agreement.

The Lord had taken all that pain away. How could I still ache so? Was it simply a desire that I still carried or a deeper problem that was hindering my healing?

I decided to ask God. He had answered my other questions and had helped me through those issues, and so I knew He would have an answer to this question too. And he did, but the answer that I received really dumbfounded me!

God revealed to me so very clearly why I still experienced the pain and why I felt such a need for more babies. It was definitely one of those Wow! moments. It is hard to put into words, but I knew as clear as day what He was trying to tell me...I wanted more babies for me, pure and simple. Being pregnant and having babies made me feel good. It was something I was good at; something to be proud of. Pumping out beautiful little children was something I could do well.

Having babies had become a competition in my mind. How many beautiful little boys could I produce?

It was sick and sad...but true.

How could having babies turn into a competition? One word: *PRIDE!*

Yes, pride had dug into my soul and had taken root when I was just a little child. I always had to do better and be better, than anyone else at everything I attempted. In a family that always loved me, but didn't always have special time for me, I had to get attention any way I could.

If I were better than everyone (at anything), I would get the attention that I so desperately craved.

Somehow, in my mixed-up mind, I decided that the ultimate game to win was to be the best mommy and to have the best babies, in fact the more, the better! I had also decided that if I could have a whole bunch of beautiful, little children, then all the sins of my past would be erased.

And that was the secret that I hadn't even told myself. Despite this, the Lord, through his miraculous grace and mercy, showed me what was causing my anguish. Once the truth was revealed, the repentance and forgiveness came and the peace began to flow!

> *For he who sows to his flesh will of the flesh reap corruption, but he who sows to the Spirit will of the Spirit reap everlasting life.*
>
> *Galatians 6:8 (NKJV)*

Now, that could be the end of my story...and the Princess lived happily ever after.

Unfortunately or fortunately (sometimes you never know) my life took a different twist.

> "Whether or not God will answer our prayers is not a matter of question, but how He will answer may leave us wondering."
>
> —Janette Oke [4]

Let us therefore come boldly to the throne of grace, that we may obtain mercy and find grace to help in time of need.
Hebrews 4:16 (NKJV)

> "A balanced woman of God sees herself as valuable, gifted, responsible for her own growth and maturity—not overly dependent on anyone to get her through life or to make her secure."
> —Charles R. Swindoll [5]

Who can find a virtuous wife? For her worth is far above rubies. The heart of her husband safely trusts her; So he will have no lack of gain. She does him good and not evil All the days of her life. She seeks wool and flax, And willingly works with her hands. She is like the merchant ships, She brings her food from afar. She also rises while it is yet night, And provides food for her household, And a portion for her maidservants. She considers a field and buys it; From her profits she plants a vineyard. She girds herself with strength, And strengthens her arms. She perceives that her merchandise is good, And her lamp does not go out by night.

She stretches out her hands to the distaff, And her hand holds the spindle. She extends her hand to the poor, Yes, she reaches out her hands to the needy. She is not afraid of snow for her household, For all her household is clothed with scarlet. She makes tapestry for herself; Her clothing is fine linen and purple. Her husband is known in the gates, When he sits among the elders of the land. She makes linen garments and sells them, And supplies sashes for the merchants. Strength and honor are her clothing; She shall rejoice in time to come. She opens her mouth with wisdom, And on her tongue is the law of kindness. She watches over the ways of her household, And does not eat the bread of idleness. Her children rise up and call her blessed; Her husband also, and he praises her: "Many daughters have done well, But you excel them all." Charm is deceitful and beauty is passing, But a woman who fears the LORD, she shall be praised. Give her of the fruit of her hands, And let her own works praise her in the gates.

Proverbs 31:10–31 (NKJV)

Through The Fire

God did not save Shadrach, Meshach and Abednego *from* the fiery furnace, God saved them while they were *in* the furnace, and He was right there with them...

I have been in the furnace, and I believe I have come out the other side, with my Lord beside me all the way.

As you have just read, a great release came into my life, during the summer of 2002, when I was finally able to forgive myself for killing my unborn baby almost twenty years earlier. Having that abortion haunted me for such a very long time.

I had spent so many years of my life reliving that event over and over, but God, through His infinite abundance and unlimited mercy, said to me, "Give it to me, I'll lighten your load"...and I was finally able to do so!

My load was indeed lightened! I was finally free of all the guilt and shame that had encompassed me for the majority of my adult life. I was finally free at last to tell my story to others and to pray that somehow, through what I was learning God would be able to help someone else.

So, I began telling my story, and it was met with

renewed blessings as I saw others being blessed by the words God gave me.

Then I woke up one day, not feeling very well at all, and realized that I was pregnant again! Oh my! God had given me a new gift; a new chance with another new life. And so, began the life of Chance Daniel Schneider.

It was not an easy pregnancy from the get go. Having previously lost two babies at around ten weeks, when I started spotting at eight weeks, I went to my first OB appointment filled with dread. I just *knew* that something was wrong and all I could think about was that I just couldn't handle another miscarriage. I really didn't think I could go through that pain one more time.

"No, God, please not again," was my constant prayer. But when that ultrasound picture came up, there was a dancing, moving, live baby inside of me and I thanked the Lord for His faithfulness and goodness to me. I truly couldn't believe I was going to be given another baby.

I called Chance my "Golden Child." The ultrasound was in 4-D and it gave such a beautiful golden picture of our little baby boy.

By the time my 12-week appointment rolled around, we were all breathing a sigh of relief. This baby was to be. He was such an active, busy baby, that my fears were replaced with dreams of all the fun he and his brothers would have together. The anticipation of adding a new member to our happy little family grew... we were all thrilled and excited and were planning the future with our newest addition!

Then one day, my world dropped out from underneath me and I found myself in the middle of that fiery furnace. It was just a routine doctor's appointment. No big deal...no problems. I was 18 weeks pregnant and halfway to my July 16th due date.

As soon as the doctor started the ultrasound, I sensed a difference in his attitude and then came the words that had bore so much pain before, "I'm sorry, but your baby has no heartbeat."

No heartbeat...what??? NO...that means Chance is dead! My baby can't be dead! I just felt him kicking! Oh, Lord, please don't let this be happening!

Please Lord, NO!!!

But, it was true. The next three days were filled with pain and numbness as I was induced into labor and delivered my tiny little baby boy on Valentine's Day, 2003.

I did not see my Chance. I could not bear to bring myself to look at him. I was afraid the memory would haunt me forever. Unfortunately, the memory of not seeing him, I fear, is much more painful than the memory I would have carried with me of him.

The weeks that followed were a blur of pain and numbness. I had learned many years ago how to remove myself from me, and the day that I delivered that little baby was so unbearably painful that I could not bear to be me any longer and so I left myself.

Oh, I was present in body, but my mind went someplace where it could endure the pain. I can't really describe it, but it is a form of disassociation. I believe it kept me from doing harm to myself, but it also kept me from healing.

And it kept me from life...from living...from being.

I stayed in that place for several months. On the outside, I appeared to be dealing with my grief. I had always been good at hiding things. I would put on my "Christian" front and pretend to be fine, but inside I was crumbling. And I would realize what was happening and make attempts to get help and some days I felt I had. I would pray and I would feel peace for a time, but it would never last long and I'd be right back in that fire...worse than I had been before.

I truly thought I was going crazy. I could not talk about it, as I did not understand it. How could I tell someone that I thought I was going crazy?

I just kept thinking to myself, *I am a Christian. I love the Lord! I have a powerful testimony of His peace and mercy with the freedom I have just experienced in dealing with my abortion issues, and now, I lose my baby and I go nuts?! What sort of testimony is that? I know the baby is in Heaven with Jesus, so why can't I let that thought bring me peace? Don't I love the Lord? Can't the Lord heal me?*

All of these thoughts, plus thousands of others kept penetrating my mind. And I had no answer.

Me...who always had an answer, who was always in control, had no clue of what to do.

Wow...talk about getting knocked off a high horse.

I remember one incident that really scared me. I had met some of my friends from church at a local park to have a play date with the kids. I remember the whole time I was there, I felt like I was outside of my body, watching them, but not really being a part of the group.

I don't think I carried on a conversation with anyone, that day. If I did, I had no recollection of it and after an hour or so, I felt, what was the point? I had nothing to say to anyone, anymore. The sad thing was these girls who I had gone to the park with weren't just acquaintances, they were my close friends. That day, however, they might just as well have been total strangers, as I couldn't find anything in my mind to talk with them about. So I gathered up the boys and drove home. I knew at that point I had two choices: I could stay the way I was, sinking into a depression that was intensifying on a daily basis, or I could try one more time to get help.

I chose to get help.

This time, I had no clue what I needed or how to get it, so I called my friend Cindy and met up with her for a time of prayer and reflection with the One who has all the answers. I believe the first step toward my receiving help from the Lord was admitting that I had no clue as to how to help myself, and that I could not do so on my own. The second step was allowing *Him* to do *His* work.

The Lord started revealing things to me immediately, and He did not stop until we had been through every gamut of my life and back again.

He started out with anger, unforgiveness, and various other things. Then He revealed to me that I had lost trust in Him. I knew in my heart that I had been *angry* with the Lord, and as hard as it was to admit that, I had not thought that I didn't *trust* Him. But God knows everything and He knew that lack of trust was a huge part of my problem.

The reason I could not stay close to the Lord was because I didn't trust him. He had allowed my baby to die. Why would my God, who loved me, allow my baby to die and cause me so much pain?

Since I had no answer, I guess in my twisted head, I decided that I would just simply stop trusting Him. I would go back to a life that I could control. I decided that since I had given my life to God and had ended up in such pain, that I would just handle the rest of it myself.

Of course this was not a *conscious* decision. I did not say to God or to anyone else, "I don't trust God. I'm going back to handling things here." But that was what was in my mind; my subconscious thoughts were handling all issues. Or should I say *not handling* them?

When confronted with this realization, I knew I had to make a choice, a conscious choice. I had to choose to either **trust** God or to **not trust** God. Wow! Do you have any idea how difficult it is to realize that you do not trust the Lord who created all things? Who can do all things? And how wrong it is to think you can do a better job? Ouch...not good.

I repented of losing my trust in God and I asked for His forgiveness. I continued to pray and seek His will in all areas of my life. It was so freeing, to simply allow God to lead and direct my thoughts. And as I prayed, a very miraculous thing happened to me. My mind, which had literally felt like it was two separate halves, up to that point, actually came back together. Right there...*right in the midst of my prayers.*

Too wild! Yes, I know it sounds crazy, but as I told you before, I was already on my way there. So at that point, not too much would have surprised me. But to have the Lord, actually put my head back the way it needed to be, while I was conscious of it...

Well...all I can say is "Thank you Jesus, You are an awesome God!" Many things came out that night...too numerous to name them all. The main thing I believe the Lord wanted me to release to Him was *control* of my life.

Since I had been a small child, I had always felt like I had to do everything myself. I was not good at asking for help. It was a burden that I carried with me my entire life.

Now, in the world's eyes, that is a good thing; being independent, being capable, being responsible, etc. And yes, we all need to have the ability to take care of our lives—don't take this point wrong. Being independent, capable, and responsible are all important traits to have in living a well-balanced life. The problem with me was that I had taken that control to another level...a level that didn't belong to me...a level that belonged to God.

God gave me back my life that evening. It's funny...as soon as I gave it to Him, He gave it back to me, but in oh so much better condition!

Sort of like the story with the little girl whose daddy bought her the pearl necklace and he asks her to give him her old necklace each day, so he can replace it with the real pearls. But she just can't part with her old necklace, so she misses out on receiving the *real* thing.

I didn't think I could give up my old life...so in the meantime, I was hanging on, and what I was hanging on to was not all that it should have been. But I was afraid to give it up, as it was all I had.

When I finally did give it to the Lord, He immediately fixed the brokenness and set me back on a path towards healing and happiness.

I asked the Lord to take away all of the junk in my life that night and to fill me up with Himself. That is what I strive for. To be filled up with Jesus! I want Him to overflow out of my life.

Do I believe that life will be a bed of roses for me now?

No, unfortunately, there is a daily battle between good and evil. I want to do good. The evil one does not want me to do good. However, I do have a part in the outcome of this journey. I need to guard my mind, my will, and my emotions against the enemy. I know from experience, he will use whatever he can to break into those places where he is not welcome.

He does not come knocking at my front door. He worms his way in through minute cracks and once he gets in, he attempts to gain control. My job is to guard the cracks. Thankfully, I now have the Lord's armor to wear for protection.

As long as I guard my heart and keep God first in my life then I have access to all that is promised by Jesus and that includes abundant life—not just being, but truly living!

I went home from Cindy's house that night and,

as I always like to validate these special times with God with His Word, I opened up my Bible. The Lord directed me to John, to the story of Jesus speaking with Martha, after the death of Lazarus. That night, God gave me these words:

> *Jesus said to her, "I am the resurrection and the life. He who believes in me will live, even though he dies; and whoever lives and believes in me will never die. Do you believe this?"*
>
> *John 11:25–26 (NIV)*

I think that says it all! Praise You Jesus!

> "To believe the truth of the gospel—that abundant life in Christ is really NOT about having it all, being it all or knowing it all, but about knowing Him through it all—is to practice authentic faith."
> —Brenda Waggoner, *Fairy Tale Faith* [6]

> *While we do not look at the things which are seen, but at the things which are not seen. For the things which are seen are temporary, but the things which are not seen are eternal.*
>
> *2 Corinthians 4:18 (NKJV)*

Now we're starting to get into the meat of my

story and actually, now that I'm talking food, this is the part where the chili and chocolate cake come in.

You see, all during the time of my last pregnancy, when I was not feeling very well, and life was going up and down like the waves of the oceans, and then after the baby's death, when the waves came crashing over the top of me, there was one stable thing in my life—Thursday night church supper. I couldn't miss it. I needed the fellowship of my friends desperately. I realized early on that trying to figure out what to take each week was an added burden which truthfully, my mind just did not want to take on.

So, I decided that I would make a pot of chili and bake a chocolate cake each week. And I did just that. I cooked weeks upon weeks of chili and chocolate cake. Weeks when I was sick from nausea, weeks when I was exhausted, weeks when the pain of my grief started to overwhelm me, weeks when my mind was numb, weeks when I knew nothing else, chili and chocolate cake were always there. And I would not miss those suppers. Even when I would go and not feel like talking to anyone, something drew me to them each and every week.

I know it may sound silly to you, but to me, those weekly dinners were my lifeline when I was drowning. We all need routines in our lives to keep us grounded, and making that weekly pot of chili was mine.

Now, I am going to share some thoughts that

are very painful for me to divulge to you. But, I truly believe that the purpose of me sharing my story is to help you, if not today, then later on in your own journey.

So many times we don't focus on our pain; we simply push it down or push it away, pretending it's not real. But it is real and it needs to be addressed.

No wound can heal until it is brought out into the open. In one of the many books I have read about grief and pain, someone shared the thought that no one actually writes about the pain, *during* the pain. Instead, most of the help books are written *after* the healing has occurred.

That is so true, because it's hard to write *during* the pain. But, I did and I'd like to share that experience with you. I feel like we're getting to know each other and that I can reveal a little more of my soul to you at this point in the game.

No, the editors didn't miss editing the following chapter. I am leaving it as it was written, so you really start to understand the depth of the pain I felt at the loss of my Chance. It's hard to appreciate the healing, if you don't get a glimpse of the wound.

> "In our desire to be an inspiration to one another we often veil what is true, because what is true is not always inspirational. But hurting believers whose lives are in tatters often need REAL help. If we were able to put aside our need for approval long enough to be authentic, then, surely we would be living as the church."
> —Sheila Walsh, *Honestly* [7]

Though I walk in the midst of trouble, You will revive me; You will stretch out Your hand Against the wrath of my enemies, And Your right hand will save me.

Psalm 138:7 (NKJV)

Blessed are those who mourn, For they shall be comforted.

Matthew 5:4 (NKJV)

Yea, though I walk through the valley of the shadow of death, I will fear no evil; For You are with me; Your rod and Your staff, they comfort me.

Psalm 23:1 (NKJV)

My Golden Child

Pain...Pain...Pain...so intense...so deep.

How could one person feel so much pain and still survive? Pain that cuts into you like a knife that digs deep into your soul. After the pain, comes the numbness. The disbelief...this can't be happening to me, no...this is a dream, I will wake up.

After the numbness wears off, the true despair begins. Because by this time, you should be on your way to 'healing' according to the world, but they don't know that you just spent the last two months in a state of shock.

Why the despair? Why can't I just accept the loss? How easy is it to simply let the pain go? Let the pain go. Let the pain go.

Oh...my sweet little Golden Child! How much I loved you. No one will ever know! I cannot describe the intense joy that I felt when I knew you were to be. I thrived on the discomfort of my early pregnancy, because I knew that the sicker I felt, the stronger you would be.

Then, the day came of that first spot, and my heart stopped. I could not believe that I had grown to love you so much and you might not make it. I just couldn't image another loss. Not you. Not this miracle baby that came from such intense release. Such freedom from the past. You were a beginning to me, a beginning free from the burdens of my guilt and my shame. You were the new life, manifested in me, and I loved you so intensely!

And I went to that first doctor visit, expecting the worse, but praying so intently that my God who loved me so much would love you just as much and protect you, and you were fine. You were kicking and jumping and leaping and I saw you, my Golden Child and the intense joy grew and grew!

Your brothers loved you, oh so much. Chase kissed my belly that was your home. He couldn't wait to see you in person, but he loved you because you were his baby brother.

And your brother Carson was so concerned that I would not do anything to harm you. He did not want me to even carry the groceries, because he wanted you so badly. He remembered the pain of losing your brother and he did not want that to happen again. Nor did I...

And your Daddy loved you, oh so very deeply. He was afraid to show it at first, afraid to reveal his love because of the pain of loss that he knew all too well, but when you were 12 weeks old, he sat in that doctor's office and watched you kick-box, and you won his heart. He fell in love with his little Golden Child.

But no one loved you as much as I did, my special Little Boy. I loved you so very much. It hurt, the love that I had for you, but it was such a special pain. I would put my hands on you every night and pray to Jesus to be with you, pray to Jesus to keep you safe and pray to Jesus that you would be His child!

And we named you Chance Daniel Schneider. And you were so very very special.

I started feeling you moving around inside of me and I was so overwhelmed with joy. I could sit for hours and just bask in your movements. And we passed all the 'danger' times and I could finally relax and just love you and dream about the day we would meet you face to face; your family who all loved you so very much.

And I dreamed about all the fun you would have with your brothers. Carson would teach you so much about the world and Chase would show you how to have fun in everything that you did. You're Daddy, would be the best Daddy in the whole wide world to you. He would teach you so much about anything you wanted to know. And you're Mommy, would simply love you. Love you with a love that knew no boundaries.

It was just a regular doctor's appointment. We were all excited to see how much you had grown, what was new with you. Your brothers were there, excited beyond words to see their little baby again. I was so calm and peaceful; I didn't even start praying that day, the way I had before every other ultrasound. I knew you were fine! I had been feeling you kicking even as they started the procedure.

But the doctor seemed very quiet when he looked at you. He made mention that you were breech. You were only 18 weeks, I thought, why would that concern him? You had plenty of time to spin around. Then came the words that changed my world, forever.

"I don't know how to tell you this, with the boys here, but your baby has no heartbeat."

He could have reached over and slapped me in the face; I would not have been more shocked. I just stared at him. What did he mean my baby had no heartbeat? That meant he was dead. He couldn't be dead. Not my Golden Child. Not my little Chance. I had just felt him kick me. He had to be wrong.

The feelings that overwhelmed me were so intense and so painful, the tears came and my mind went blank. What was I to do? What about my baby?

How ?? Why??? What ????

Somehow I got to the car in a semi-conscious state, but once behind the wheel, away from that office, the tears flowed, the pain wrenched out of me in agonizing moans. My poor boys did not know what to say or do. Chase thought I was laughing and he did not like the sound and he said over and over again, "Stop it Mommy." Carson understood something was terribly wrong and he tried to calm Chase down and all I could do was lean on the steering wheel and sob. Huge, gut wrenching sobs.

Unbearable Pain...so much pain...

"Your baby has no heartbeat." "Your baby has no heartbeat." "Your baby has no heartbeat."

Three different times I have heard those words. Three different times my world has stopped.

Not again Dear Lord...Please, Please, Please, God...NOT AGAIN!!

The drive home was a blur of tears and sobs and pain...of so much pain.

And a brain that would not function any longer.

How could my world get turned upside down with 5 little words???

What was I going to do now? How could I tell Bobby?? How could I go on??? How could this happen???

Constant thoughts...no thoughts...constant tears...no thoughts...so much pain!!!

I didn't know what to do, I call Cindy. She would know. She would help me. Help...Please God...Help me!!

How can I tell Bobby??? How can I do this again...?? So much pain!! So much confusion!! How could my Golden Child be gone?? God why??? Why???

You gave him to me??? Why??? Why the pain??? Why the pain???

Chili and Chocolate Cake

My friend, Cindy, comes and the tears won't stop. The pain is so intense. How can my baby be gone?? Why??? Why???

Help me...God Help me.

And then there is Bobby...oh no...not again. I can't bear this again. I can only lean on him and cry and cry and cry. No words will come. Nothing but tears and pain.

I am falling into that abyss...God help me... please help me.

There are decisions to make and I cannot make them. I have no thoughts. My mind is not working and I cannot think. I do not know what to do. I am a machine now, simply following my instructions. I cannot think. I cannot think. I do not know what to do.

God Help Me! God Please Help Me!!

The day is a blur of doctors and hospitals and pain. Always the pain. On the surface, trying to deal, trying to make some sense out of this, going through the motions.

I have to be induced into labor. Is there no end to this pain??

The labor starts and it comes fast and intense. At least now the pain is physical. And it can be numbed.

Two percocets and the physical pain is gone, but what can I take to kill my mind? What can I do to stop my thoughts???

God, where are you?? Why is this happening

to me? I love you!! I know you love me. Why are you allowing this pain? Why??? Why???

The hospital is a blur...give me everything you have. Anything to numb my pain. I don't want to be here. I am not here. I am somewhere else. This isn't me. It can't be happening to me.

What? My baby is just going to 'pop' out? No please no. No, there is nothing I can do. Wait...wait...wait...

All night waiting. What??? Give me what?? More drugs, more pain. Now I am physically sick...oh well.

What does it matter?? What matters any more??

It is not me that this is happening to. I am having a bad dream. I will wake up and say, "WOW, that was horrible." Thank you God it was only a dream.

But I wake up and there is a strange nurse and a strange doctor and they are telling me to push. They are pushing on me and pulling on me and where is Bobby?

Where is God??

No one is here with me.

And than out comes my baby.

I feel him slipping out of my body and there is nothing I can do to get him back. He is gone...gone...gone...

They put my little baby boy in a metal pan beside my bed. And they cover my little baby boy up with a

Chili and Chocolate Cake

bloody towel. And that pan sits there and sits there and sits there while they continue to push and pull at me.

I cannot deal with it. I am gone now. My body is still lying there, but my mind has gone away, somewhere where it is not so painful, away from this place.

I cannot bear to see my baby. How can I not see my baby before they take him? How can I see him? What will happen to me if I see him?? What will happen to me if I don't???

Give me more drugs. I cannot deal with this any more. I cannot be here any longer. I cannot think another thought.

I sleep...and sleep and sleep. And I cannot think.

Bobby comes to take me home. He brings the boys. It is Valentine's Day and they bring me candy. They do not understand. They do not understand.

How can I eat candy?? My baby was just ripped out of me?? How can I go on when my baby was just ripped out of me???

I cannot deal with this...God Please help me??? God where are you???

On the surface. . .motions. . .inside. . .nothing. Nothing but pain.

My Golden Child is gone. I did not even get to hold my baby and he is gone.

I loved him and he is gone. Gone...Gone...I didn't even get to hold my baby and he is gone now.

Oh Lord, Help Me. Help Me. Please God.

Too many phone calls...too many people to try to tell this to. It's just a dream and I'll wake up. I am going through all the motions, but I am not really me. I can't handle the pain. I cannot do this. God Help ME!! Please Help Me.

It has been 10 weeks since I lost my Golden Child.

You would think the pain would be less. It is some days. And some days it isn't.

It has been a terrible roller coaster ride. A constant battle.

Physical - Emotional - Spiritual.

Everyday a different enemy. Every day a different struggle. But always the same Victor. Thank you Jesus!!

Do I believe that God took my baby? No.

Do I believe that God could have kept my baby safe? Yes.

Do I understand any of this? No.

Do I still love the Lord?? Yes.

Am I happy? No.

Will I be happy someday?? Yes.

Do I think this pain will last forever ?? No.

I believe that I have no control over my life as it stands. I only know that I have control over my thoughts and I have to keep my thoughts focused on the one who can pull me through this. If I allow myself to slip, I will never come back.

> Father...I don't know why my life has taken all these flips lately, but I know that you are here and I know that you will lead me forward. Father I do not want to go back into that abyss...that pit. Lord, Please... Please Help ME!!
>
> I love you Lord!!
>
> > In Your Son's name, the name of Jesus, I pray!
> > Amen
>
> *Thank You Jesus for answering my prayers. Hallelujah!! Thank you Jesus!*

The Journey Back

"I'm dying," were the only words that I could utter following the loss of Chance. Death was all I could think about...the death of my baby, the death of my dreams, the death of my mind, the death of my thoughts.

I also experienced the death of my joy, the death of my happiness and the death of my peace.

Did I experience the death of my faith? No...not the death of my faith! Thank goodness!

Even when I couldn't pray, I could say, "Please help me! Help me not to go crazy. Help me not to lose my mind. Help me not to let this ruin my life. Help me through this, Lord. Help me through this, Lord!"

Our God is truly an awesome God and He did help me.

Mine has been a journey full of lessons that has given me a greater knowledge of Him and His love for me. It has also been a journey that has shown me, once again, that alone I can do nothing, but that with God, there is nothing I cannot do!

The beginning of the journey was first full of intense pain, then denial, then numbness—that distancing or removing myself from myself, so as not to feel the pain.

God was good to me during that time, however, and supplied me with such a great abundance of His peace, that I did not do damage to myself despite the fact that I had no control over my thoughts. Thank you Lord!

Of course without acceptance, there cannot be healing.

There was a surreal quality to those days—an appearance of normalcy, yet knowledge inside that things were not as they should be. I did not truly understand, yet was very willing to just continue living the status quo where the pain was dulled and bearable.

Life was not easy during that time, as my emotions seemed to take on a life of their own. I seemed to be on a fast moving roller coaster ride, with no control over the highs and lows that were coming at a increasingly faster and faster pace!

Then one day...BOOM!!! I was hit with such grief and such pain! Where had that been hiding??

I believe it was there all along, but it had been pushed down into a place that I didn't want to visit. After all, what if the pain caused me to blame my God? I couldn't blame God for this. I loved God and He loved me. He would not let this happen to me.

And when the pain and the grief surfaced, my natural instincts were to numb them away. Wasn't that always the answer before? But, I knew in my heart of hearts, it wasn't the answer this time. Oh, it was a struggle. Don't be fooled. It was a terrible struggle, but God came out the victor! He led me to a book that started a thought process in my mind, and that allowed truth to surface and healing to begin. The book was *If God Is So Good, Why Do I Hurt So Bad?* by David Biedel.

I did have anger towards God. It was hindering my walk, but I was afraid to admit that. I thought being angry at God was wrong. How could I admit to God that I was mad at him? He is the God of the Universe. I had no right to be mad at Him, so I pushed my anger down inside of me and tried to get on with my life, but it wasn't working.

The pain kept growing and the grief kept resurfacing, and my emotions were on their own wild, careening course heading straight for disaster.

Then one day, the truth came out. It was a very simple truth, but it was truth nonetheless. I finally said to God, "God, I am mad at you." Surprisingly, I felt God tell me that it was okay, that I was His child and that sometimes children get mad with their parents and that it's natural. I had gone through a terrible loss and although I did not *blame* God for it, I also knew in my heart that He could have prevented it, because He is God and He can do anything.

I am thankful that I believe that God can do anything. Even during the most difficult times I knew that I still believed in Him and I still loved Him. I was just angry at Him.

I asked God to take away my anger, my sadness, and my pain and to replace them with His great peace and His never-ending love. God is so faithful—He did just that. He took away all my anger, sadness, and pain in such a very peaceful way. He did not drag them out of me, He simply said, "Rest in me. I will carry all your load."

God picked up that baggage and took away my burdens; so very simple, yet such a process to attain.

WOW!

I am healing. I don't feel terrible grief or pain or sadness today. I can think of my little baby Chance, and the picture in my mind is of the day we all saw him dancing and kick- boxing and having a big time, and the day his Daddy fell in love with him.

My little "Golden Child" is in heaven with my Lord.

"I am alive!"

Thank you, Jesus!!

I had a lot of scattered thoughts during that time...I am so reminded of it by the words from Jeremy Camp's song- "I Still Believe" [8]

> Scattered words and empty thoughts
> Seem to pour from my heart I've
> never felt so torn before
> Seems I don't know where to start
> But it's now that I feel your grace fall like rain
> From every fingertip, washing away my pain.

I still believe in your faithfulness
I still believe in your truth
I still believe in your holy word
Even when I don't see, I still believe.

I know you are probably wondering why this particular time in my life gets so much attention. Well it is because this was a giant turning point for me. It was the lowest of my lows, but it also became the highest of my highs. *It changed my entire being.* Until you know the extent of the wound, you cannot truly understand the miracle of the healing.

So bear with me...here's an e-mail I wrote to a good friend during this time that gives you a little more insight into what I was going through:

Hi Mary,

I have been given more of God's blessings and His peace through another very intense time of seeking God's face and His answers. I'd like to share my experiences with you.

On Sunday, I had a terrible grief attack. I'd had a baby blues week all last week, as Chase has been on a home video kick and wanted to watch movies of himself and Carson as babies. I really wasn't into seeing those movies, but I also didn't want to deny Chase his fun, and he does love them so much. I didn't sit and watch them with him, but I did see a lot of them and they were really special. But when I saw the scenes of Carson and Chase as newborns, in the hospital, that terrible memory of Chance just came crashing back to me.

As a result, all week long I had been dealing with baby issues: grief, emptiness, sadness, and yes, even hope for another baby.

Chance has rarely been out of my mind since that day I delivered him, but I have had various levels of peace about him. To me, peace is not going out of my mind. Peace is not wanting to drown my sorrows in alcohol. Peace is not lying in bed all day. Peace is not living on Valium or sleeping pills. Peace is not wanting to run away somewhere and hide from my life and from the world around me.

God's peace has kept me from doing all those things. But God's peace has not taken away the fact that I wanted that little baby desperately, that I loved him intensely, and that he was ripped away from me. And God's peace has not taken out of my mind that horrible day that I delivered him.

On Sunday, Michele and Dave brought their new baby to church, and although my mind was extremely happy for their joy and blessings, my heart started to break seeing that little, tiny baby. The vivid images of my last scene with Chance were not pleasant, and that is the image that kept flooding my thoughts.

Laying there in that hospital bed, all by myself, and having that doctor and that nurse, pushing and pulling on me, and then Chance coming out, then all the blood, and putting him in that metal tub and covering him up with that bloody towel was more than I could bear. It was like something died inside of me that morning. I felt like I had exited my body at that time and that it wasn't really happening to me. It was someone else going through that.

During the past few months I have been dealing and surviving on the surface, yet I have not really allowed my true hurts to come out. The pain and grief inside of me has been all-consuming. But on Sunday morning, when I saw that new little baby, I couldn't deny the pain any longer, even to myself. All the horrible images of that terrible day when I lost Chance began playing over and over again in my mind.

All Sunday afternoon, those images haunted me. I spent the day in bed, crying and depressed. I left for Bible study, intending to ask for prayer to help me overcome those horrible scenes that would not leave my thoughts.

But when I got to Bible study, I discovered that Michele and little Amy had come as well. There was no way I could discuss my problem with Michele there — she was so happy with her new little angel. That would not have been fair to her. That was her first visit back to Bible study in months, and I couldn't ruin it for her.

So I prayed for strength throughout the study and was about out of there, when I caught the eye of one of the girls, and she realized I wasn't okay.

Megan followed me out to the parking lot, and I just broke down, crying desperately for my baby and the terrible loss I was feeling.

I cried all the way home and was met at home by a phone call from Cindy, asking what was up. Not really able to explain why I was so upset, we decided to meet for prayer and see what God would reveal to me.

Monday was a miserable day for me. I could not fight off the depression and defeated spirit that had overcome me and the worst part of it was I just didn't care anymore.

I began to feel myself falling back into that dark pit that I had spent so much time in before, but this time I wasn't fighting the battle. I was letting the darkness envelop me and was slipping further and further away from the light.

The crazy part of this was that my anger at the Lord was not an intentional, "I'm mad at you God!" In fact, I really didn't even realize it was happening. I knew something was wrong, but I just didn't know what it was. I hadn't denounced God or my faith, but both were slipping away, and I was too caught up in my grief to even realize the seriousness of what was occurring.

I had an ominous feeling of dread when I was heading to meet with Cindy for prayer; almost like there was a black cloud over me, and it followed me right into church that morning. It was like I knew there was something seriously wrong, but I couldn't put my finger on what it was.

But God is truly an awesome God, and He knew what my problem was and what was needed to fix it.

As we began praying, God started to reveal to me that I needed to put my focus on Him...that the desire to have another baby had actually become my god. I was consumed by that desire, and it had become first in my life.

A few weeks prior to that I had been driving and thinking about Chance, and God had revealed to me that that was how much He wanted me to love Him; He wanted me to love Him as much as I loved my babies! He wanted to be first in my thoughts. At the time, I thought I did love Him the most, that He did come first, but obviously that was not true.

As Cindy and I continued praying, God revealed to me yet another piece of the puzzle that held the answer to why I could not get past the desire for more babies. I had thought the issue stemmed from my abortion and never being able to forgive myself for it, but God showed me something new, a thought that had never occurred to me before.

I was lonely. I wanted babies to fill up my empty spaces.

Before, I had used drugs, alcohol, and men to fill the voids in my life, but those were not options any longer. Having babies, however, was. Again, this truth was revealed so that I could make myself right with God. He wanted to fill my empty spaces. He wanted me to allow Him to supply all my needs.

> *And my God will meet all your needs according to his glorious riches in Christ Jesus.*
>
> *Philippians 4:19 (NIV)*

I needed to repent of not putting God first and of letting my desire for a baby rule my emotions. I needed to let my little Chance go. He was with God now, and I had to let God's peace back into my life and let His healing take away my pain.

At some point in time, I had let the enemy slip into my life, through tiny little cracks, and he had begun to take root in me and feed me the lies that were allowing me to plunge back into the darkness. He hadn't come knocking on my front door, and I hadn't welcomed him in, nonetheless, he was there. Although I did not understand, or even fully comprehend, I knew something was desperately wrong and that I had some serious choices to make:

> Choices between life and death...
> Choices between peace and turmoil...
> Choices between God and flesh...

I went before the Lord and this was my prayer:

Thank you, Lord, for your gift of discernment.
Thank you, Lord, for showing me the right choice.
Thank you, Lord, for revealing to me the root of my turmoil.
Thank you, Lord, for allowing me to once again come and rest in you.

AMEN

Mary, I am believing that the Lord is going to deliver me and that I am going to receive victory in this battle for my mind! It is a battle that I so desperately want to win...Thank you so much for your prayers and your concern for me during this time. I value our friendship greatly!
Love,
Joyce

> "Our lives may have turned out so vastly different from the vision we once had, and yet fresh reminders of God's grace reach down through generations of flawed, frail human love, not wiping out our problems, pain, and disappointments but loving us through—and beyond—our limitations."
> —Brenda Waggoner, *Fairy Tale Faith* [9]

In this is love, not that we loved God, but that He loved us and sent His Son to be the propitiation for our sins. Beloved, if God so loved us, we also ought to love one another. No one has seen God at any time. If we love one another, God abides in us, and His love has been perfected in us.

I John 4:10–12 (NKJV)

Where To Go Now?

I'm not even sure what I want to say at this point, I am simply allowing the Lord to lead me. If you have lost a baby, please, know that it *does* truly matter to God. He grieves with you. So many times people will try to say all the right things to try to comfort you, but the words are not a comfort.

It *doesn't* matter if you have ten healthy children; you *still* wanted that little baby.

Yes, it *may* be nature's way of taking care of the baby, if there was a physical problem, but in your mind, the baby *was perfect.*

Yes, you *may* be able to have other children, but it *still hurts!*

Yes, you *know* the baby is in heaven with Jesus, *but you wanted him/her here with you!*

Please don't try to hide the pain or bury the hurt. Allow yourself the time to grieve. One of the worst things I did was to try and put a timeframe on how long I was "allowed" to feel sorrow. Only *you* can answer that question. Take as much time as you need to get through this process.

Find a friend you can talk to about this and talk... talk it out, until the hurt starts to heal.

If a friend loses a baby, here are the best two words you can offer, "I'm sorry."

If you have suffered the loss of a child through miscarriage, stillbirth, or at any time after you gave birth to them, I am so very sorry. May the grace of God fill you up, and may His peace wrap around you like a warm comforter.

> *Blessed are those who mourn, For they shall be comforted.*
> *Matthew 5:4 (NKJV)*

Six months after I lost Chance, I was still undergoing the healing process and was working to keep my life moving forward.

Around that time, I felt called to start a Bible study for the moms of our church. We had already been getting together once a week for the kids to play and we decided we might as well utilize our time and implement a study for us while the kids had their playtime. One morning at study, God taught me another lesson which I will share about in the next chapter.

That is one of the things that I have been learning—you can find a lesson in every situation or experience, if you simply look for it, or allow God to show it to you.

It's a challenge some days, to learn the lesson, but it's always worthwhile!

Father God, I thank you that even when I don't "feel" your presence, you are with me. Your Holy Spirit lives within me and never leaves me. My emotions can leave me feeling dry and empty, but Your Word quenches my thirst and fills me up. Please, fill me up more, O Lord.

I love you Jesus.

In Your name I pray,
Amen

And Jesus said to them, "I am the bread of life. He who comes to Me shall never hunger, and he who believes in Me shall never thirst."

John 6:35 (NKJV)

Gain Through The Pain

On one particular Friday morning during the prayer request time of the ladies Bible study that I had started, we were supposed to share a request regarding a personal issue...not just a "generic prayer." Ouch!

There I was, leading a study group of Moms, supposed to be setting a good example, and yet I didn't want to share the one burden that was *still* consuming my soul!

As the girls started to share their requests, I scurried around in my brain, trying to think of something easy to say, like, "Pray for Carson in school" or "Pray for wisdom in my mothering," but those were not the issues that invaded my thoughts each and every month.

I knew what I needed to ask prayer for, but would I really do it? Then, it was my turn...

I sat there, a bit open-mouthed with nothing coming out. I started to say something meaningless, then all of a sudden I blurted out:

"Oh, I really need prayer about the situation with Bobby and me not having anymore babies. We don't use birth control, and Bobby was supposed to look into getting a vasectomy after we lost Chance. He hasn't done anything about that issue yet, and although in my heart I still want another baby, I am scared to death to actually get pregnant. Every month I go through severe emotional trauma, wondering, "Am I, or am I not pregnant?"

Please pray that I can talk to Bobby about this situation. It is just so difficult that I won't bring it up, but every time I don't, I'm forced to go through the monthly emotional roller coaster all over again."

One of the girls prayed for my request. Three or four days later, I happened to notice that it was close to time for me to start my period. In fact, if I went by my new schedule since the loss of Chance, I was actually late.

Oh boy, not this again, I thought. Of course, once you start thinking of the situation, it intensifies and every feeling becomes magnified, and then you aren't sure if you are starting the beginning of a PMS symptom or if you are experiencing the beginning symptoms of pregnancy. The symptoms are so very similar...so very much the same, but oh, such different results!

I counted the days, and counted the days again and tried to figure out what was what, but I had no answer, because I had given that part of my life to the Lord, no longer knowing the *right* day to become pregnant. I encouraged myself to just wait, but the signs of pregnancy increased, and with no signs of a period coming, my thoughts turned more and more to the idea of being pregnant.

I was scared to death! Being pregnant had always brought the image of my beautiful little babies, so small, yet so special with such intense joy! But this time the only images that flashed through my mind were doctor's offices, ultrasounds, hospitals, and pain.

NO, NO, NO!!! No more pain, Lord! Please, Father!

I couldn't bear the thought of nine months of such stress, and I wouldn't even allow myself to think about losing another baby. Losing Chance almost put me over the edge. I was there for a while and there was no way I could even think about going back to that place!

I fell to my knees and I prayed. I prayed for the Lord's comfort and I prayed for His peace because I knew that this was one journey I could not take alone.

And although the thoughts still consumed me, they were not as scary as they had been previously. I was comforted knowing that I would not walk the journey alone.

Even still, I couldn't bear to tell Bobby. He was so busy at work, and he had so much on his mind, I couldn't tell him that we were about to go through this journey...again.

"I will just wait," I thought, "but, if I don't tell

him, he will not know what I am going through. He will not understand the emotional roller coaster that I ride every month. He needs to know…but I don't want to tell him."

I waited and I waited and then finally, I blurted it out one night while we were preparing for bed. "I'm sorry to ruin your mood, honey, but I think I'm pregnant."

Ouch…maybe I could have been a little more gentle? But by this point, I was getting comfortable with the idea. I had a few days to pray and my mind was settled on the thought that I was pregnant.

Bobby's reaction was just as I had expected. I had totally burst his bubble. Now, I should explain a bit more about my husband here. Bobby is the world's greatest Daddy and he loves Carson and Chase more than life itself. But losing Chance had been so difficult on me and for him, that he did not want to risk going through another loss. He was very content with our two sons and although I dreamed of a houseful of children, he did not share that dream.

Bobby had grown up with a large family and he had always felt pushed aside for the new babies as a child. He always felt that his parents never had any time for him, and he had no desire to carry that burden into our family. I had tried and tried to convince him that not all families were like that, that we could love more than two children equally, but having more babies was *always* a sore subject with Bobby and me.

"How? Why? Oh?" he would say and then would come the silence, the silence that always followed those conversations. The silence that I have grown to despise. The silence that had created such a chasm in our relationship. The next day, we had our confirmation. I was back on my normal schedule and was therefore not pregnant. We all got another reprieve.

But...there was always next month, and the month after that and I didn't know how much longer I could allow myself to go through such turmoil. Waiting for confirmation was an extremely intense emotional exercise, one that drained me each month and consumed my thoughts.

So I ventured forward, and asked Bobby the question that I had requested prayer for in my women's Bible study the week before, "What are we going to do?"

Although there were no clear answers, that day, the lines of communication were at least opened and conversation started to move freely as thoughts and suggestions were brought up. We actually had a *discussion* on this oh, so sensitive subject: the subject that had haunted our marriage since day one. In fact, this subject, this issue of babies had haunted our lives since even before marriage, when I didn't care if we were husband and wife, but I so wanted us to be Mommy and Daddy.

For over ten years, we had never discussed this matter in any comfortable forum and finally, we, as a family, (yes, even the boys were involved in this conversation), allowed our thoughts and ideas to flow freely!

Oh, my "Thank you, JESUS! Thank you for your freedom! Thank you for your love! Thank you for your answered prayer."

No...we did not come up with a solution that day. But the subject was at least opened so that discussions could follow. The most important thing through it all was that God was leading us.

In the song, "I want to know you...," we ask God to show us who He is. I believe I saw who God is that day...*God is love!*

God wanted to answer my prayer regarding Bobby, but I had to take that first step. Until I did, nothing could be resolved! So, I ended up in a situation where I had no choice—I had to talk to Bobby about it. And as soon as I did everything else started falling into place.

At that point, I had to purpose myself to pray more and to seek in what direction the Lord would have me continue. I had to work to keep the lines of communication open between my husband and I and I had to seek where the Lord was leading. Fortunately, the peace of the spirit brought me much gain through my pain and turned my pain into peace.

Thank you, Jesus.

> "I know that God is faithful. I know that He answers prayers, many times in ways I may not understand."
> —Sheila Walsh [10]

And whatever things you ask in prayer, believing, you will receive.
Matthew 21:22 (NKJV)

Call to Me, and I will answer you, and show you great and mighty things, which you do not know.
Jeremiah 33:3 (NKJV)

And whatever you ask in My name, that I will do, that the Father may be glorified in the Son.
John 14:13 (NKJV)

Well, as you can see, there is never a dull moment in my journey, especially in the battle for my mind. It is always something. But what I am learning through the process is the key, and believe me, having a walk with the Lord is a *process.*

I read a really great book the other day entitled,

Having A Mary Heart In A Martha World, by Joanna Weaver. In it, she talks about "our journey to faith." "... Christianity is a process and not an event. It is a journey, not a destination," [11] she tells us.

Isn't that the truth? How many times do we rush through life, trying to get to a destination only to find out we missed the whole trip getting there?

I know, in my situation, I was spending all my time grieving the loss of what I did *not* have, when I had some very special people right in front of me. God had given me a wonderful husband and two beautiful little boys, but I could not see the forest for the trees...I was so caught up in my pain and grief that I was failing to recognize all that the Lord had blessed me with.

Then one day I read a book that really seemed to sum up a lot of my issues in one simple truth—I wasn't really being *real.*

This book, *The Velveteen Woman,* by Brenda Waggoner seemed to be written just for me, right where I was.

Shortly after reading it, I summarized the book and led a discussion on it at a weekend retreat. I'd like to share those thoughts with you in the following chapter. Although my thoughts cover the concept of the book in a nutshell, I'd encourage you to read it in its entirety. It will touch your heart.

> "God has a wonderful plan for each person...He knew even before He created this world what beauty He would bring forth from our lives."
>
> —Louis B. Wyly [12]

For I know the thoughts that I think toward you, says the LORD, thoughts of peace and not of evil, to give you a future and a hope.

Jeremiah 29:11 (NKJV)

Being Real

What does it mean to be real?
Have you ever pondered that statement?
   Are you a:
   ...real person?
   ...real wife?
   ...real mother?
   ...real Christian?

In this increasingly materialistic world we live in, sometimes we actually forget how to be *real* or even what *real* really means!

In this chapter, I want to focus on being a *real* person, a *real* Christian, and how to have a *real* relationship with God. I believe that when you start to grasp this concept, you will become more *real* in every aspect of your life.

In the book, *The Velveteen Woman,* Brenda Waggoner tells us that "Real is...a thing that happens to you." [13] She explains to us that *real* is something we become gradually, as we face life vulnerably, returning to God over and over and finding ourselves loved, even when life hurts, when it doesn't make sense, and when we're angry or afraid.

Brenda's book title and thought concept is adopted from the classic children's book, *The Velveteen*

Rabbit, written by Margery Williams. In the child's story, which begins on Christmas morning, The Velveteen Rabbit, is a new toy a little boy receives for Christmas. The boy is thrilled with his new bunny and plays with him for all of two hours, before getting side-tracked with other new toys and gifts. The bunny is placed on a shelf in the boy's playroom and forgotten.

At night, when the nursery magic happens, the toys begin to move and talk. Some of the other toys snub the bunny, but the old, wise Skin Horse is kind to him. One day the Rabbit asks his friend, "What is real?"

The Skin Horse, the wise old man of the nursery, replies, "Real isn't how you are made, it's a thing that happens to you. When a child loves you for a long, long time, not just to play with, but REALLY loves you, then you become *real* [italics mine]."

The Rabbit asks if it hurts to become *real.* "Sometimes," the Skin Horse answers, since he is always truthful. He goes on to explain that becoming *real* doesn't often happen to those who break easily or have sharp edges or have to be carefully kept. Bit by bit, the Skin Horse has learned to rest in the transforming love of his master, knowing this is what he was made for.

In *The Velveteen Woman,* Brenda tells us, "As women, we will have a myriad of experiences—some pleasant and some painful—as we journey toward *Real,* [italics mine] to that place of comfortable authenticity with God, with ourselves, and with others. There will be fragile moments of crisis when we feel as though we might break easily, other times when our perfectionism demands we remain 'carefully kept.' Times when we feel afraid to ask questions, intimidated, confused, or even put on a shelf, forgotten. Through it all, we long to be known, to be loved, to become more *Real,* [italics mine] but we'd prefer it not take a long time or hurt too much." [14]

In his book, *If God Is So Good, Why Do I Hurt So Bad?,* David Biebel tells us, "In relation to faith, 'real' isn't magical, though it is supernatural. And it is uncomfortable, the result of merging the pain of living with the joy that knowing Christ can bring into a unique message that only you can give and that only He can energize." [15]

Wow...the merging of the pain of living with the joy of knowing Christ. What a powerful statement!

Life can be painful. Sometimes it seems like we cannot really grasp the fullness of God's love, what a *real* relationship can mean...until we reach a place in our lives where we have nowhere to turn but to God. He can take our brokenness and restore us to a place of peace and love and yes, even joy!

In *The Velveteen Woman,* the author's brokenness and subsequent faith journey came when her husband of fifteen years asked her for a divorce. Instead of facing the pain, she stuffed her hurt and anger down inside, and instead of being honest, she resorted to a numbed religiosity, pretending to be strong, while inside growing doubts and anger towards God bubbled away.

Because she was a Christian, she felt like she had to forgive her husband and not face the anger and hurt that was inside of her. She opted for the "Land of Pretend," the place where everything was neat and tidy, and where there were no real problems or pain. Not understanding the consequences of a make-believe life, she missed the chance to live in the "Land of Real."

It took quite awhile before she allowed God to break through her exterior of perfectionism and convince her that what He'd wanted all along was the REAL Brenda—doubts, fears, questions, faults, and all.

She explains that to be *real* is not always pleasant; it is not light dinner conversation, and you cannot unmask your pain with every acquaintance. However, if you are unwilling to settle for superficial spirituality, you must learn to first be honest with yourself and with God. You then need to find someone who you can trust to be open and be vulnerable with, someone who you will allow to love you through your pain, and someone who will walk with you to the "Land of Real." Becoming *real* happens slowly, bit by bit. It is not an overnight occurrence and unfortunately, it is not something that is altogether in your control. "Real is a thing that happens to you." [16]

The book tells us, "One of the methods God uses to interrupt our religious recitations is to allow a crisis into our life's drama. Often, this crisis opens the door to growth and freedom, however painful it feels at the time." One of the author's friends said it so well: "A crisis can force us from a starring role in 'Let's Pretend' to spontaneously playing a God-directed part in 'Being Real.'" [17]

My journey towards the "Land of Real" didn't occur the day I prayed the prayer to receive Christ. Yes, that was a start. As a new believer, I wanted to believe that God really loved me, but I didn't love myself because I was carrying so much baggage from my past.

As I was able to start stripping off the layers of my past and actually get down to who I really was in Christ, God's love started becoming more and more evident to me.

And then I lost Chance and the "Land of Pretend" became my home, because I could not face the pain. I had lost the little baby that I believed had been given to me from God. While I was pregnant with Chance, the pain of my past with the abortion and all those years of guilt was gone, and my hope was renewed because I was going to have another chance with a new life.

When that little baby died, the pain was more than I could bear.

Because I was a Christian and I loved the Lord, I wanted to say, "It is okay...my baby is in heaven." *But it wasn't okay! I did not want my baby in heaven. I wanted him on earth with me!*

I was afraid to say that to God. I was afraid God would reject me if I told Him how mad I was that Chance was gone, and how much pain I was experiencing. I didn't know it was okay to be mad. I didn't know it was okay to really hurt. Instead, I put a smile on my face, said I was okay, and went on about my business. Even though I pretended to be okay, I didn't live a *real* life. There was too much pain bubbling up inside me.

Pain cannot heal when it is pushed inside. It festers and it simmers, but it does not go away. It cannot go away until it is brought out into the open to heal. But I couldn't bring the pain caused by the loss of Chance out, because it hurt too much. So I left it inside, where I thought I could deal with it.

However, eventually the pain *had to* come out, because there is no life living in the "Land of Pretend." Bobby deserved a *real* wife and Carson and Chase deserved a *real* mother, so I finally allowed God to begin His healing process in me.

Now, God wanted to heal me all along, but He could not do it until I *received* His healing. It took concentrated effort on my part. Once the healing process began, I believe I really started to understand how to be *real* with God. He didn't want the "pretend Joyce." He wanted the *real* me...hurts, doubts, fears, anger... *everything!* He wanted to wrap His blanket of peace around me and comfort me, really comfort me.

In *The Velveteen Woman,* Brenda Waggoner tells us that in our human nature, it is hard to grasp the depth of God's love. He loves us regardless of what we do. He loves us regardless of whether we experience success or failure, whether we are on good behavior or bad behavior, and even whether we are obedient or disobedient. God's love for us does not change. His unconditional love is hard to fathom in a world filled with "conditions."

God is the true author of unconditional love. In our small minds, it is so hard to fathom a love so fierce, so far-reaching, a love that concerns itself with our well-being, even when we are faithless. He endures our faithlessness because He just refuses to stop loving us.[18]

His love is our gift. He loves us...just because!!

God calls people to faith, not certainty, yet we as humans, want a father who gives us certainty. We want all the answers and we want them *our way!* Conversely, God wants us to trust in Him, to return to Him over and over in the midst of life's ups and downs, to face up to life as it is instead of pretending how we think it should be. Faith is not the same thing as denial of reality. Faith has more to do with being fully aware of life as it really is, yet letting go of control and believing God will handle all the areas of our lives. It's saying, "I'm scared," when I feel afraid, instead of saying, "I'm fine." [19]

It's saying, "This past year was really crappy, probably the worst year of my life, yet throughout it all, I have more peace and feel closer to God than ever before! God is so good!"

God wants our laughter, our tears, our dreams, our fears, and our hearts! He wants all of us!

When we compare ourselves to others, we always lose. We aren't spiritual enough, pretty enough, thin enough, smart enough, rich enough, etc...

To God, we are all precious. He loves each and every one of us in a way that is beyond compare, and by accepting His love for us, we can shed that feeling of, "I'm not good enough," and become the *real* person that God wants us to be.

In I John, chapter one, John gives us an excellent example of walking in the light. Light is a place of exposure, a place where you *have to* be real, because you cannot hide.

John says this is the place where we experience fellowship with God and with each other. He also says that when we walk in the light, the blood of Christ cleanses us from sin. This is because sin cannot be cleansed until it is confessed or admitted:

> *If we confess our sins, He is faithful and just to forgive us our sins and to cleanse us from all unrighteousness.*
>
> 1 John 1:9 (NKJV)

In his Gospel, John says the reason people won't come to the light is because they want a covering under which they can hide their sin.

> *And this is the condemnation, that the light has come into the world, and men loved darkness rather than light, because their deeds were evil. For everyone practicing evil hates the light and does not come to the light, lest his deeds should be exposed. But he who does the truth comes to the light, that his deeds may be clearly seen, that they have been done in God.*
>
> John 3:19–21 (NKJV)

Okay...now it's time to get REAL!

What is in your life today that is keeping you from being *real?*

What pain have you pushed down inside that you don't want to face?

Maybe it's the death of a parent? Or a bad relationship with a sibling...

Or a husband who cheated on you...

Or problems with money...

Or the loss of a child...

God wants to take that pain from you and start you on the *road to real* today!

Take some time now and get *real* with yourself. What is it that is holding you back from having a *real* relationship with God? What is keeping you from allowing Him to direct your path?

> *Your word is a lamp to my feet and a light to my path.*
>
> *Psalm 119:105 (NKJV)*

Never brush your teeth with beauty lotion...

Although the container MAY look like toothpaste, it does not taste like it and it probably does not have the same effect.

Being Humbled

After I gave my talk on *The Velveteen Woman* to the women at that retreat, I felt so very holy and spiritual. I thought I finally had all the answers and that God had completed His work in me. But you and I both know that the Lord is never finished with us, don't we? God revealed yet another new truth to me later on that evening.

You see, all during this time of pain and grief, I had felt abandoned by my husband. Now, he really didn't abandon me, but I needed someone to blame, and since I couldn't blame God, well, Bobby was the next best thing.

I blamed him for leaving me alone in the hospital the morning Chance was delivered, even though I told him to go, that I was fine. (It was Valentine's morning at Carson's school and I had sent him home early to get Carson's valentines ready and get him off to school.) How was he to know the baby would come while he was gone?

I blamed him for making it so difficult for me to talk to him about losing the baby. Every time I would bring up the subject, he would quickly change it—he never wanted to talk about Chance. I blamed him for us not having any more babies. In fact, in my mind, I felt Bobby was to blame for all my pain. Somehow, his not wanting more children had caused all this to occur, in my thoughts.

Now, I never discussed this with Bobby. Instead I just started resenting him, and as a result, our relationship started to disintegrate. We didn't fight or argue. On the contrary, we rarely talked. Bobby did his thing and I did mine, and I was very comfortable with that scenario.

But then God showed me that weekend, at that retreat, that I wasn't being *real* in my relationship with Bobby. God showed me that I held resentment towards him and I that needed to release it and to ask his forgiveness.

Ladies, I don't know if you have ever had to ask your husband for his forgiveness, but I can assure you, it is *not* an *easy* thing to do. I was thinking, *Lord, anything but that. Please don't ask me to go talk to Bobby about this. He just doesn't understand and I don't want to go there with him any longer.*

But God wants us to communicate with our husbands; He wants us to humble ourselves when we are wrong.

So...humble myself, I did. Boy, that was absolutely no fun. Having to tell Bobby that I blamed him for my messed up mind. But, God knows best. Bobby was so very gracious, loving, and forgiving and he made the situation very easy for me. He made it much easier then I deserved...but isn't that how God works? He doesn't give us what we deserve; He gives us His love.

> Father God, I have so many questions and so few answers. Reveal to me Your will. Show me Your path and give me the wisdom to follow it. Feed me Your word, Lord. Educate me in Your ways. When the questions of life are confusing or overwhelming, remind me to wait on You, the One who has all the answers.
>
> I love you Jesus.
>
> In Your name I pray,
Amen

You will show me the path of life; In Your presence is fullness of joy; At Your right hand are pleasures forevermore.
Psalm 16:11 (NKJV)

You would think that by this point in the story all my issues would be resolved and my happily ever after would *finally* have begun. Isn't that the life you thought of for yourself when you were dreaming of being grown up? A family, a nice home, and good friends? Well, I have all of that and so much more. So what happened to the *happily ever after?* Where had it gone? Why did I not feel happy? Why was I still not getting it? Oh...I'd get it for a while. I'd be content for a time. But eventually, the junk would come creeping back into my mind, invading my thoughts and controlling my life.

It makes for a good story, but living it is a bit of a challenge. But as I said earlier,

Christianity is a journey, not a destination, and it's most certainly a process.

> "God may not provide us with a perfectly ordered life, but what He does provide is Himself, His presence, and open doors that bring us closer to being productive, positive, and realistic."
> —Judith Briles [20]

...add to your faith virtue, to virtue knowledge, to knowledge self-control, to self-control perseverance, to perseverance godliness, to godliness brotherly kindness, and to brotherly kindness love.

2 Peter 1: 5–7 (NKJV)

Friendly Advice

Ladies, always empty your bladder BEFORE jumping on a trampoline, especially if you have experienced childbirth.

Modern Day Miracle

Recently, one of my friends posed the question, "Do we believe that God can do miracles today?"

Since the Word says, He is the same yesterday, today and forever, then my answer was, "YES!"

A lot of healing that God gives us is not of the *make-me-well-immediately* variety, although He can and does enjoy providing this gift to us, but rather healing our broken hearts and restoring our minds when the enemy has planted his seeds of deception and lies within us.

In early February of 2004, God gave me a miracle. He raised my spirit from the dead. I really wasn't sure why I was struggling, but for about a week or so, I did not feel right within.

It was nothing I could really put my finger on. The first anniversary of the loss of my little Chance was fast approaching, and to make matters worse, I had delivered him on Valentine's Day. This wonderful, special holiday of love, was to me, only a reminder of the terrible pain I had experienced in losing that special little baby.

To add to the pain, a baby shower was being planned by my friends from church for a first-time mom, and again, a very special time of love, was only to me a huge source of pain.

In my past dealings with pain, I had chosen to simply ignore it and to let it fester, so I decided I would take the same route this time, and just choose to ignore both Valentine's Day and the baby shower.

But, on that day in early February there was no ignoring the deadness of my spirit. My joy was gone, my peace was nowhere to be found, and the pain was overwhelming. I felt that old blankness start...that *Why bother?* feeling that has plagued me so much in my past.

"NO!"...I kept thinking. I cannot go there again, but when you are there, it's really hard to understand how you got there, so the confusion of what is happening adds to the overwhelming feelings that start to haunt you, leaving you more bewildered and deeper into the enemies snare.

I *knew* God could help me, but I wasn't sure I could do what I needed to do to receive His healing at that point in my journey. What else did He want from me? I had given him all I had; I had emptied my soul to Him and to the world...what was left? I didn't know.

Now, that is actually just the place where God wants us to be...the place where we do not know and all we can do is turn to Him!

I decided to send out my Daily Prayer, something I had been doing for quite some time. I would mail out a daily thought/prayer/story to a group of online friends and family, a daily devotional to lift them up and encourage them, a bit of truth from The Lord. I thought maybe that would help. I shuffled through my books looking for something good to send, but nothing was connecting. Then I saw it—a quote from Ralph Waldo Emerson [21]:

> "What lies behind us and what lies before us are tiny matters compared to what lies within us."

"Hmmm," I thought. This is me.

I always let the past play into my mind, I let the pain and the grief back, and I couldn't stop thinking about what was to come.

The quote from Ralph Waldo Emerson really got me thinking. Those issues are tiny compared to what is within me.

Then I thought to myself, *Well what is within me?*

I started thinking about that and realized that what was in me was so much more powerful then all the other junk my mind kept returning to. *The Lord of all creation lives within me! How cool is that?*

A little bit of God's peace settled in. That was good. I then found a verse to relate to these thoughts:

> *And we know that all things work together for good to those who love God, to those*

who are the called according to His purpose.

Romans 8:28 (NKJV)

I do love Him, and I have been called to His purpose, so whatever is going on in my life, I had to believe that God would work it for good.

A little more peace settled in.

I then decided I really needed to get one-on-one with Him, and for me, that meant immersing myself in praise and worship music.

I put on "He Is Yahweh" [22] and let the words and the music bring me to Him.

> Who is moving on the waters?
> Who is holding up the moon?
> Who is peeling back the darkness
> With the burning light of noon?
> Who is standing on the mountains?
> Who is on the earth below?
> Who is bigger than the heavens?
> And the lover of my soul?
> Creator God: He is Yahweh
> The Great I Am: He is Yahweh
> The Lord of All: He is Yahweh

As those words started filling my soul, the sobs started, and the pain and grief poured out of me, as He filled me up. He filled me up with His comfort and His peace. He turned my bitter into sweet! God is so very,

very good. He showed Himself to me in a very special way that day—He gave me a *modern day miracle.*
Thank you, Jesus!

> "In our darkest hours, when we need God most and can't understand why he doesn't help us or answer our calls, He's somewhere out there beyond the range of vision, rearing up and growling at the evils in our lives in ways we'll never be aware of."
> —Brenda Waggoner, *Fairy Tale Faith* [23]

No man shall be able to stand before you all the days of your life; as I was with Moses, so I will be with you. I will not leave you nor forsake you.
Joshua 1:5 (NKJV)

But the story isn't finished yet. Actually, I doubt it ever will be until I go to be in Glory with my Lord. The really neat part of this story has been and continues to be, that God has revealed His Will to me, and is walking with me step-by-step through my healing and learning process.

He did not give me all my lessons in one day or even one week or even one month. They were spread out over a very long period of time, where I could learn and digest and draw closer and closer to Him through a gradual process.

We don't marry someone after the first date because we don't know them well enough to take that step of faith with them yet. The same is true of our relationship with the Lord. He asks us to take that first step towards Him, and He takes a step towards us. And step-by-step we move together, overcoming the hurdles that the enemy continually throws in our paths.

The wonderful part is we are not alone through this journey. Jesus is right beside us every step of the way, and some days He even has to carry us, as we are too weary to continue on. But take heart, He tells us:

...I will not leave you nor forsake you.
Joshua 1:5 (NKJV)

So many times, we may feel like all we have to do is pray the prayer and we will have this instant, magical faith. But real faith doesn't work like that. When we ask Jesus into our hearts to be our Savior, God has given us His promise of salvation, at that time. It is ours, but what follows next, the growing in His Spirit, well, that is the process, *the journey.* And that my friend, is truly where the true joy resides!

And so the story of my journey continues...

As I wrote this book the topic of prayer was often on my heart. One day God gave me a great revelation and I would like to share it with you now:

We pray for all our needs, we pray for health, we pray for family issues, etc., and we always want God to grant our requests, to give us what we ask for.

When He doesn't, we think He hasn't answered our prayers, that He doesn't care about us, or that He is ignoring us.

But what we must realize is that **NO** is an answer.

Sometimes the answer to us is **NO**. Wow...here we are, as little children, praying to our Heavenly Father, asking and asking and asking, but not realizing that He has already answered our prayers, and He told us, "No...that is not for you at this point in time."

Now, I'm sure many of you have already learned this truth, so bear with me...it's just so much fun for me to learn truth that God reveals to me personally. Thank you Jesus!

Chili and Chocolate Cake

Father God, thank you for answered prayer...whether you answer yes or no to us, we know that You only have our best interest at heart. We know that we don't know the end of the story, so we can only trust You in directing our paths.

Lord, thank you that we have an open flow of communication...that You want to abide in us and that You let us abide in you. You want to come into our hearts and You want us to come into Your heart. And Lord, in doing so, we are able to become more like You, which will enable us to do the tasks that You instruct of us...sharing You with others. We love you Lord!

In Jesus' name I pray,
Amen

It shall come to pass That before they call, I will answer; And while they are still speaking, I will hear.
Isaiah 65:24 (NKJV)

The Lord is far from the wicked, But He hears the prayer of the righteous.
Proverbs 15:29 (NKJV)

Call to Me, and I will answer you, and

show you great and mighty things, which you do not know.
Jeremiah 33:3 (NKJV)

He shall call upon Me, and I will answer him; I will be with him in trouble; I will deliver him and honor him.
Psalm 91:15 (NKJV)

Friendly Advice

When using a food grinder to grind a product that turns into liquid (example: tomatoes) be very careful NOT to put too many tomatoes into the grinder at one time, EVEN if the lid is larger and you THINK it could accommodate them.

It won't...in fact, it could become quite messy.

Wrestling With The Enemy

John 8:32 says, *And you shall know the truth, and the truth shall make you free.* (NKJV)

Wow, how cool is that verse? We shall know the truth, and the truth shall make us free! I recently learned yet another truth and I believe it has set me free from yet another issue. I know, I know, you're thinking, "There's more?" Believe me, I feel the same way.

Since the day I lost Chance, I had felt that a part of me had died. In fact, those were the first words I said to my friend, Cindy, on the phone that first night, when I called her, "I'm dying."

Throughout the following days, I proceeded to die inside a little more each day. Yes, there were good days and bad days and days of trying to overcome the struggles and days that I didn't care and I let the struggles overcome me. During those times, the pain and the grief were too much to bear, so I escaped them by stuffing them down inside of me into a place where I could live with them, but I could not heal from them.

As I talked about earlier, I realized several months after the death of my baby that the life I was leading was not going to work. I realized that I could not continue living in that *I don't care place,* in the "Land of Pretend." I had turned to the Lord and He had gently led me out of the pit and back to reality. Unfortunately, back in reality, the pain and the grief still remained. Oh, it wasn't a throbbing pain, but rather more like a dull ache, just under the surface, waiting to erupt!

And erupt it would. Sometimes it would be a simple, *I want my baby* thought, and the tears would flow. Sometimes it would be that *It's not fair* issue and the green tongue of envy would lick at my mind. Sometimes it would be much heavier. News of a new pregnancy would *always* cause that intense pain to come cascading back, flowing over all my rational thoughts and throwing me down into that pit of despair. I experienced despair for my loss and pain and grief so intense that it would overpower all other thoughts, requiring me to start the battle back, once again.

> *For we do not wrestle against flesh and blood, but against principalities, against powers, against the rulers of the darkness of this age, against spiritual hosts of wickedness in the heavenly places.*
> *Ephesians 6:12 (NKJV)*

I *hated* the battle. I wanted to stand firm, but for whatever reason, the enemy constantly invaded this area of my mind, and it was a continuous struggle to stand firm against him. It would take two to three days of relentless prayer to climb up from that pit and continue on, when one of these attacks occurred.

The battle was scary and the pit was deep, and I always worried, *What would happen if the next time, I didn't climb out? What if I got stuck down there?*

This was *not* a place I wanted to be, and this was *not* a place God had ordained for me. So why couldn't I overcome it? Why couldn't my faith, through Jesus Christ overcome this battle?

I had no clue, but I knew who did; and one day I decided it was time to find out.

The Lord had always been there to reveal His will to me in the past, so I figured He would be there once again. *After all,* I wondered, *What could possibly be hidden inside of me that hadn't been brought up and out before?* I had no clue and truthfully, I was almost afraid to find out.

So I prayed...but there seemed to be a block. I could not receive what God was trying to show me. All I could see was the pain, and I *knew* that was not from God...

God reveals things to us using many different vessels. Sometimes it's through His Word, sometimes it's through prayer, and sometimes it's through others.

This time, my revelation came through a friend who had always been there to help me in any way that she could. For whatever reason, this time I was not able to see my problem, or hear about it from the Lord, but my problem was becoming quite clear to her, and because she took that leap of faith and spoke it to me, I was able to see it as well.

The issue was not neat and tidy, but rather complex and a bit messy for me to understand. Basically, I had developed an unhealthy bond with Chance during my pregnancy. This was partially due to Bobby's lack of excitement towards the baby when we first discovered that I was pregnant, and partially due to my pure excitement over having another baby—something which I had wanted for a very long time. I had just gone through that huge release from the freedom of my abortion when Chance was conceived, and I believe in my mind he took over the place of that first little baby. He was truly my second chance!

Whatever the reason, from the first moment that I knew he was to be, Chance was very special to me and not just special in an "I'm having a baby" way. **Chance became my world.**

And when he died, a part of me died with him. So anytime the topic of babies came up, I did not remember the joy of delivering Carson and Chase, but rather the pain and the grief that had dwelt in me since Chance's death.

Another issue that was hindering my healing dealt with old feelings of insecurity and insignificance that had somehow reared their ugly head back up inside of me.

I had always struggled with these issues as a

child and through my school days; but I felt after I was out in the *real* world, those issues were long gone. But for whatever reason, they were starting to surface again, and into them had somehow entered the issue of having children and being a mom.

Somehow, I had started basing my significance in life on my ability to be a mom—I thought that if I had more babies that I would be more significant. I had dealt with an issue very similar to this before involving pride and babies, if you will remember, and I think it must not have been totally released, because it came back tenfold with little Chance.

Another huge hindrance was that I had stopped communicating with Bobby, again. I was still blaming him for all our baby issues, for not wanting Chance to begin with, for not supporting me during the early weeks of my pregnancy when I was so sick, for not being with me in the hospital when Chance was born, and for not wanting to talk about him after his death.

I had tried a few months before to get this out—I had even asked Bobby to forgive me for this stuff—but low and behold, I realized I had not forgiven him!

I had put up a huge wall around my relationship with Bobby, to the point where I still loved him, but I wasn't truly interested in much that he did. I had a terrible *Whatever* attitude where Bobby was concerned. He could do as he pleased, as long as I was left out of it, I just didn't care.

Now this is a horrible place to be. Bobby and I had been best friends for years! We had never had a problem communicating, but this baby issue had gotten the better of us and it was affecting every aspect of our life together, and really starting to create a huge chasm in our relationship.

Here I was in this place, struggling desperately with pain and grief, not being able to communicate these struggles with Bobby, and wondering what in the world God was going to do to help get me out of this mess. Isn't that just the way we work, too? We make the mess and then we expect God to fix it for us.

But God, being a loving God, so much wanted to help me. He gave me a revelation that I needed to *forgive and forget. Forgive* Bobby for all the blame that I had placed upon him (much of which was ill-placed, to say the least) and then *Forget* about all of it.

JUST LET IT GO!

Hmmm, now that was not an easy request, but once God revealed to me, through the words of my friend, this idea of *misplaced significance,* it all started to flow in my mind.

How in the world, could I let the idea of someone else being pregnant, determine my own significance? That was a ludicrous idea, to say the least, but it hit the nail right on the head. Somehow I felt like, in losing the baby, I had lost my significance! Then, on top of that was the fact that every time a new baby image came to me, all that flooded my being was the pain and grief that had flowed through me during my loss.

So, if I could change my thought process, then, when those times would occur, instead of resorting back to pain and grief, I could process those thoughts for what they really were...joy for another, new life for another family, a blessing to them...thoughts all about them...*not about me!*

I had to realize that having a brood of children would not make me more significant. My significance can only come from one thought...*being a child of the King!*

To gain significance from anything else is wrongful thinking and will lead to trouble. I am a Child of God. He loves me *for being me,* not for anything that I have done, or will do. *He simply loves me because of who I am.*

That love is so comforting....it is a warmth that spreads over me from head to toe. In being loved by God, I don't have to be on top of the mountain happy every second of the day, but rather filled with the contentment of knowing that I am the *Child of The Most Holy One!*

In changing this thought process, God also allowed me the courage to confess these issues to Bobby, to tell him everything that I was experiencing, regardless of what I perceived his reactions to these thoughts to be. I shared it *all* with him. That conversation enabled Bobby to show me that the marriage vows we took together almost nine years earlier were still very important to him.

"For better or for worse..." Well, I was definitely *for worse*. Poor guy. Having to deal with my emotional ups and downs was, as he put it, "Like dealing with a ship being tossed in a storm." He had no clue what to expect from me from one day to the next, and although he was having a hard time communicating his support, he continued to show it with his steadfast love.

Once God helped me break through those communication barriers, I was able to share with Bobby why I was acting the way I was, and he was so willing to help me in whatever way he could. God gave me back my best friend that weekend. Thank you Jesus!

This huge communication breakthrough actually occurred while Bobby and I were out on our date for Valentine's Day. As I told you earlier, I had planned on skipping the entire event, due to a general lack of interest, but God had other plans. He encouraged me to go out with Bobby, to rekindle the spark, and to let Bobby in on what was going on with me. I listened to the Lord's gentle urgings to go out with my husband. I followed them and that evening Bobby and I not only became friends again, but our communication brought us back to the place that we needed to be, as husband and wife.

And just to be sure I was learning my lesson I actually got a test that very night!

After our dinner and discussion, Bobby and I decided to stop by a restaurant that was very special to us. It was where we had met. We had both worked there for several years, had a lot of old friends there, and we thought this would be the perfect night to stop by and say hi to the old gang.

At the restaurant, Bobby and I ran into one of our friends, who informed us that she was once again, expecting. Now, the really crazy part of this story is that with her previous two children, I had been expecting both times as well. But she has a very healthy 3-year-old little girl and a very happy 1-year-old little boy, and I just have memories of pain and loss.

Always before, news of a new pregnancy would throw me down into the pit, immediately, but this time, when I heard the news that she was pregnant, none of the pain or grief surfaced. **ZILCH! NONE ! NADA!** In fact, I was actually very happy for her, but thinking, "Wow, is she going to have her hands full now!"

I felt such an honest, open reaction to her news, which was something that had escaped me for much longer then I even care to admit. This time there was no pain, but Bobby, knowing how a statement like that could throw me, asked immediately upon leaving the restaurant how I was. It felt so good to tell him that I truly was **OKAY**!

Now, I don't profess that I can conquer this battle in my own strength; in fact, I know that without the Lord in me, I can do absolutely nothing. I've fallen down too many times to believe differently. But I do believe that God allowed my mind to start to process these baby issues in a new way, a healthy way, a way to allow healing in.

I honestly did not know if I was going to experience a miraculous, instantaneous healing. I wanted it to be so, and passing that first test was definitely a great start. But I also knew that I had an enemy who was prowling around like a lion, looking to destroy me.

> *Be sober, be vigilant; because your adversary the devil walks about like a roaring lion, seeking whom he may devour.*
> *1 Peter 5:8 (NKJV)*

Sometimes, that attack seemed relentless. I knew that the devil was not happy with the newfound freedom that I was experiencing. I had to continue to stand firm on God's Word and believe:

> *And you shall know the truth, and the truth shall make you free.*
> *John 8:32 (NKJV)*

Now I'm free in Christ Jesus!
AMEN!

This revelation was the big one! It was the piece of the puzzle that had been missing for so long. I was finally starting to get it. I could really forgive and forget the wrong attitudes I carried towards Bobby. I could finally put God in the number one spot in my life! My whole world started turning around.

I started to feel like the underdog who was *finally* starting to gain ground in the race. Not that this is a race to my faith, but face it, you've been reading my story.

Two steps forward, three steps back. It got a bit discouraging some days. And you are just reading about it. Try living it.

I wanted to overcome my flesh, to allow the Holy Spirit to rule my life, but *wanting* and *achieving* are two different things.

Don't get me wrong, *I am still not there yet,* but Praise God, I am so much farther than I've ever been!

And that is what Paul encourages us...

> *Nevertheless, to the degree that we have already attained, let us walk by the same rule, let us be of the same mind.*
> *Philippians 3:16 (NKJV)*

This verse really hit home with me one day when I was struggling and beating myself up. Paul wasn't encouraging me to be Mrs. Superstar Christian, he was simply saying, "Don't lose the faith you already have."

That is so important. We see our brothers and sisters in Christ and we think that they are such perfect Christians; that nothing ever bothers them, and we beat ourselves up because we feel like we aren't like them or we're not good enough for God.

Yes, God wants our goodness, but our goodness will not get us to heaven. Our faith in our Lord Jesus Christ is our ticket to the Kingdom!

So when you are having a bad day, and you think you are the only Christian that struggles...take heart! You aren't...God still loves you! In fact, I believe that when we are struggling, God loves us even more!

God loves us because in our struggles, we turn to Him, and that is what He desires. He wants us to depend on Him. It is when we are the most vulnerable that God can do His thing in us!

> Father God, I know You want me to experience life fully and abundantly. Forgive me for grasping to meet my own needs, and holding on to my fleshly desires. Lord, I open my hands and my heart to you, to let go of what I have, so I can take hold of what You want to give me.
> In Jesus' name I pray,
> Amen

And I will give you the keys of the kingdom of heaven, and whatever you bind on earth will be bound in heaven, and whatever you loose on earth will be loosed in heaven.
                          Matthew 16:19 (NKJV)

And my God shall supply all your need according to His riches in glory by Christ Jesus.
                          Philippians 4:19 (NKJV)

Not that we are sufficient of ourselves to think of anything as being from ourselves, but our sufficiency is from God.
                          2 Corinthians 3:5 (NKJV)

And He said to me, "My grace is sufficient for you, for My strength is made perfect in weakness." Therefore most gladly I will rather boast in my infirmities, that the power of Christ may rest upon me.
                          2 Corinthians 12:9 (NKJV)

Friendly Advice

When mixing a powder and a liquid; for example, a protein shake, be sure the lid is on the container very well BEFORE you begin shaking it.

Also be sure the container is sitting on a solid surface.

Failure to secure both of these issues can result in some serious cleanup time.

Find Your Purpose

Thankfully, not *all* of my lessons with God are so intense or so painful. Sometimes they are just little bumps in my journey. God knows the extent of what we can handle, and He's been extremely gentle with me lately.

Thank you, Jesus.

I do believe that when we see God working in our day-to-day lives, even in just the little things, that it brings us that much closer to Him.

I recently went camping one weekend with Bobby and the boys. Although camping is not quite in my comfort zone, I was attempting to stretch and grow, so that I could grow closer to my family and share special memories with them. Since Bobby and the boys love camping, I decided I needed to make an attempt to share in their joy of the great outdoors.

The camping trip was for two nights, but I really felt like one night and part of the next day was enough for me to bond with them. A night in the tent, a canoe trip, and I was ready to head back home. The camping time itself had been a bit trying, as this particular weekend the campsite was at a very busy RV park, and there were tons of people to contend with in a very small area.

Chili and Chocolate Cake

Instead of falling asleep to the sound of nature, I lay awake most of the night, listening to the roar of RVs, Harleys, and folks partying. Not exactly the great, wild outdoors, but with a tent and a campfire, the boys were happy, so I made the best of it.

The next day, however, after returning from our ten mile canoe trip and having a bite to eat, I decided to make the venture home. Now, at some point in life I seem to have developed a driving phobia, and thus I am not all that comfortable with venturing out too far. I can handle my daily errands around town, but for some reason, the Interstate is just no fun for me any longer.

Now, add to that the fact that I had to drive Bobby's truck home, (a 1987 Blazer), and that I had developed a pounding headache which seemed to encompass me once I got out of the canoe. Needless to say, I was feeling just a bit apprehensive about getting home, and I wanted to get the drive over with as soon as possible.

I asked the fellow camping beside us what the quickest route back to Naples was, as I was already envisioning a nice shower and a nap to catch up on the sleep I had lost the night before.

He assured me that a right on Route 72 and a left on Route 761 would get me to the Interstate in no time, and then Naples was just a hop, skip, and a jump from there.

I kissed my boys goodbye, told them to have fun the rest of their time, and jumped into Bobby's truck, eager for the comforts of home and my bed.

I found Route 72 very quickly and was getting excited that I was heading home with no issues and feeling confident that I had had a special bonding time with my family. As I traveled, however, I saw a Route 661 and a Route 769, but there was no Route 761 to be found.

Sure that it was just around the next bend, I drove on. After about 45 minutes of nothing—no towns, no roads, no nothing, I was starting to get a bit concerned. Adding to my headache, I also had to go to the bathroom and there was just no place for me to stop out there—nothing but a stretch of road, with high marshes on both sides.

At that point fear began to start setting into my mind (on top of the pounding headache) and I began to realize that I was going in the totally wrong direction. I thought to myself, *What should I do?* I knew I could try to find a place to turn around, but I already had at least 45 minutes under my belt and that it would take me another 45 minutes to an hour, just to get back to where I had started.

So...knowing I needed help, I called my friend, Heather. Now, my cell was almost out of batteries and my charger was in my truck back at the campgrounds with Bobby, so I was praying that I could find her and find her quickly.

Heather answered my beep immediately, and I asked her if she was near a map and if she could find Route 72 West and see where I was heading. With some help from her father, Heather assured me that I-75 was straight ahead of me and that I just needed to continue on. Well, I have to say, I did not *feel* like continuing on. At that point, I felt like giving up. I wanted to stop and call Bobby and cry and have him come rescue me. But I had to get that truck back to Naples, so I knew I had to follow Heather's instructions and continue on.

I drove for another half hour or so, and finally, I did come to I-75. I was in Sarasota...*still* 100 miles from Naples. The fellow who had given me the original directions had said that the route he was giving me was about 65 miles to Naples.

By the time I reached I-75, however, I had already traveled for over an hour and I still had 100 miles of Interstate to travel, plus, my head was still pounding. I have to tell you, there were moments in those 100 miles, as I was chugging along and those giant semis came barreling down on me, that I wanted to panic, pull off the road, and stop, but I knew I would never get home if I gave up.

So...I continued on.

And I did make it home, a little tired and a lot weary, but in one piece. Despite my less than pleasant experience, God did show me a wonderful lesson through this:

It is so easy in life to take the wrong path, to head in the wrong direction. When this happens, we need to first realize that something is wrong, then, we need to ask for help from someone who we can trust to guide us back on track.

We can't go on our feelings, we need to go by our faith and trust in the person who is leading us whether it be God Himself, or someone He puts in our path to help us back on course.

To take it one step further, when I got home, I had to call Bobby and tell him to not take Route 72—that he would get way off track if he did. I told him instead to take a route that I had seen from the Interstate that I knew would take him where he needed to go. He did, and he made it home in less than half the time I did.

The lesson: It is our responsibility to share our experiences with others, in order to help them not take the same, wrong paths.

To tie it all together, while traveling down that wrong road that day, at one point, in the midst of my frustration, I cried out, "Lord, what in the world is the purpose of this? Why am I so lost?" Not five minutes later, around the bend was a little country church in the middle of nowhere, and on its sign were the words, "Find Your Purpose in Life."

Our purpose is to be a witness to the world,

to share Jesus' love with others, to lift each other up when we fall, and to help each other stay on the right paths.

Thank you, Jesus, for once again reminding me of my purpose. There are times when I feel so overwhelmed and out of control with life. I don't know what to do and I begin to panic. Please bring Your love and Your peace to my spirit and help me to remember that it is You who is in control of everything in my life and in this world. Father, help me to just let go and allow You to do Your will within me.

In Jesus' name I pray,

Amen

But you shall receive power when the Holy Spirit has come upon you; and you shall be witnesses to Me in Jerusalem, and in all Judea and Samaria, and to the end of the earth.

Acts 1:8 (NKJV)

You will keep him in perfect peace, Whose mind is stayed on You, Because he trusts in You.

Isaiah 26:3 (NKJV)

Peace I leave with you, My peace I give to you; not as the world gives do I give to you. Let not your heart be troubled, neither let it be afraid.
John 14:27 (NKJV)

Be anxious for nothing, but in everything by prayer and supplication, with thanksgiving, let your requests be made known to God; and the peace of God, which surpasses all understanding, will guard your hearts and minds through Christ Jesus.
Philippians 4:6, 7 (NKJV)

Winning The Battle

I don't profess that the war is over. We have a very determined enemy after us, but I did win one major battle one morning that I'd like to share with you.

As I mentioned to you earlier, I lead a Mom's Bible Study on Friday mornings, and on one recent Friday the subject of childbirth and delivery cropped up.

Now, usually at the first sign of this discussion, my anxiety would start and those terrible feelings of pain, grief, and sadness would encompass me. I would soon be on my way into that pit, then struggling for days to claw my way back out. It wasn't that I wasn't happy for other's joys; I simply had too much pain in my memory banks to be comfortable talking about newborn babies.

Every conversation would bring back visions of no heartbeats on a sonogram, or that terrible day when I delivered Chance, or numerous other bad memories for me, all relating to a loss, not a gain. But this day was different. I actually even chimed in a time or two in the discussion, telling a bit about the delivery of Carson or Chase.

Wow, I was thinking, *this is pretty cool. I can*

Chili and Chocolate Cake

almost feel normal having this conversation that has been such a heavy burden for me in the past.

Then one of the girls started talking about her premature baby and how small she was and how she fit right into the palm of her husband's hand. *Oh no...*I thought, *here it comes.* And then whoosh!! I was suddenly flooded with feelings of sadness and despair. It's amazing how fast the enemy can come in and rip your joy right out of your very being.

Immediately I felt my spirit fall, and my mind pictured little Chance. I hadn't seen the baby, but I had been given a tape measure of his size and knew he fit right into the palm of my hand. I struggled through the next few minutes, but I knew I had to do something, and I had to do it quickly. I was failing fast at holding myself together.

I excused myself and walked outside and into the ladies room. I knew that Satan was trying to steal my joy. I also knew that he had no control of my life, unless I allowed him in and I had already decided that wasn't going to let that happen any longer. I told him that I was a child of the King and that he had no control over my mind or my thoughts. I told him that Jesus had tromped on him once and that He'd tromp on him again, and that I was winning the battle. Then I walked back into my study, and as quickly as my spirit had fallen earlier, it rose right back up in my soul! By the end of the study time, I had totally forgotten that I had even suffered that incident in the beginning of the morning.

Now, this may sound a bit frivolous to you, but I can assure you, when something like the issue that I have been dealing with has control over you, it is serious stuff. That day, I made my choice. I was **not** going to allow Satan to have any power over me, any longer.

I won that battle because I had Jesus on my side, and I chose to allow Him to take control that day. I didn't try to hide what was happening or stuff it down inside. I faced it head on. And together, we won!

Father God, help me to live, one day at a time. Help me to overcome the cares of this world: the stress, the worry, the anxiety, and to live as you would have me, in Your will...leaning on You for my strength. Let me truly "give it all" to you, in action, not just in words. O Father, show me how to let go. I know you have so much more for me than I can even begin to fathom. Let me receive your will in my life!

I love you Jesus.

In Your name I pray,
Amen

Therefore I say to you, do not worry about your life, what you will eat or what you will drink; nor about your body, what you will put on. Is not life more than food and the body more than clothing? Look at the birds of the air, for they neither sow nor reap nor gather into barns; yet your heavenly Father feeds them. Are you not of more value than they? Which of you by worrying can add one cubit to his stature? So why do you worry about clothing? Consider the lilies of the field, how they grow: they neither toil nor spin; and yet I say to you that even Solomon in all his glory was not arrayed like one of these. Now if God so clothes the grass of the field, which today is, and tomorrow is thrown into the oven, will He not much more clothe you, O you of little faith? Therefore do not worry, saying, "What shall we eat?" or "What shall we drink?" or "What shall we wear?" For after all these things the Gentiles seek. For your heavenly Father knows that you need all these things. But seek first the kingdom of God and His righteousness, and all these things shall be added to you. Therefore do not worry about tomorrow, for tomorrow will worry about its own things. Sufficient for the day is its own trouble.

Matthew 6:25–34 (NKJV)

Casting all your care upon Him, for He cares for you.

I Peter 5:7 (NKJV)

When you lie down, you will not be afraid; Yes, you will lie down and your sleep will be sweet.

Proverbs 3:24 (NKJV)

A Child's Heart

I so love it when the Lord answers our prayers with a yes, and He shows himself to us in such little ways, but they make all the difference in the world. I especially love it when He shows himself to the boys. One day not too long ago, Carson had his first Boy Scout/Tiger Cub Pinewood Derby Race. The night before the race we prayed that his car would do well in the race.

Well Carson won his den race and came in 2nd overall in his pack. He got two trophies. For a seven-year-old little boy, that is very exciting. That night, when we were praying before bed, I remembered that we had prayed about the race the night before, and I mentioned that to Carson. He said, "Yes, Mommy, and I prayed today at the race too."

He had mentioned to Bobby earlier that he had prayed to God for his car to win, and it did. I can hardly believe that the God of the universe can care about who wins a little pinewood derby race, but I *can believe* that he cares about my little boy.

Another incident where God revealed Himself to Carson occurred when Carson kept complaining of a choking sensation in his throat, always at bedtime. Bobby and I tried to figure out if he was having a reaction to a certain food, or if maybe the toothpaste he was using was bothering him. But we could never pinpoint a certain substance, based on the sensation that Carson was experiencing.

After about two weeks of this occurring, I decided to bring Carson up to our Pastor after a service one Sunday to have him pray for healing for Carson. He anointed Carson with oil, and told him that if he believed, as the Bible instructed, that God would hear his prayers and would heal him. Then we prayed. Carson never complained of the choking sensation again. What a wonderful gift God has given Carson, by showing Himself to him at such a young, yet impressionable age!

I had another neat experience one day where God used Chase to show Himself to me. I had been struggling through another difficult time and I went to sleep one night, imagining myself curled up on the chest of Jesus, with Him comforting me, with His hands holding onto my face, just letting me know that He was there and that He truly did love me.

Well when I woke up the next morning, I had the actual sensation of my face being held in someone's hands. I was a bit freaked out at first, because I thought I was all alone in bed—I knew Bobby had left for work earlier. When I opened my eyes though, there was my tiny little Chase, with his hands holding my face, not saying a word, just comforting me. He had never done that before and he has never done that since, but that morning, Jesus showed Himself to me through my little boy.

I don't know why God chooses to reveal Himself to me in some of these really special ways, but I am so very thankful that He does. He continually gives me a little more of the puzzle, shows me a little more of who He really is each and every day!

Another very special event happened in early August of 2004. On one Saturday night, I prayed that the Lord would guide me to be the best mother that I could be for Carson and Chase. (One of my heart's desires is for my boys to love Jesus.)

The next day, during the Sunday morning service, our Pastor was inviting everyone to a baptism of a new brother in Christ, and encouraging anyone who hadn't yet publicly acknowledged their relationship with the Lord, to do so at that time.

Immediately Carson asked Bobby and I if he could be baptized. Now, I didn't want to discourage him if he truly felt the calling of the Lord to be baptized, but I also didn't want him to go through the process, just to "do" it. I explained to him a bit about the purpose behind baptism and he was still very confident that he wanted to be baptized. I also told him that he would have to speak with Pastor Rick, as Rick would want to be sure that Carson understood the reason behind the event.

Now Carson is a very normal seven-year-old little boy. He is not that eager to perform in church nor is he particularly interested in discussions with adults, so for him to want to be baptized and agreeable to speak with Pastor Rick, I knew he must be serious.

And he was. After a few minutes of chatting, Pastor Rick assured us that Carson was aware of what baptism was really about and was ready to move forward.

And so my little boy "took the plunge" so to speak. It was such a precious sight for me, seeing him confess his love for Jesus in that way.

Before going to bed, we always spend some time talking, praying, and rubbing backs, and Carson is usually very open during this quiet time before sleep. I once again told him how happy I was that he had given his life to Jesus and thought I'd double check one more time to be sure he understood what had happened.

I asked him if he understood what Pastor Rick had said and he answered yes, that Jesus was God's son and that he believed that. I then asked him if he had asked Jesus into his heart and he gave me a resounding "YES." And we prayed. After prayer, I told him that it would be good for him to say a quiet prayer to the Lord each night after we prayed. He asked, "Everyday?"

Oh boy, I thought, *here's where I need that wisdom from Jesus.* I then asked him to think about how much he loved his daddy and how excited he was when he got home from work everyday so that he could to talk to him. And then I explained that God was his Heavenly Father and that God loved him just as much as his daddy and that God wanted to talk to him everyday too. And Carson, with the matter of factness that only a little boy could muster said, "Okay."

Carson is a "black and white" kind of person. He likes to know the answers to his questions. He can go on with "why's" for a very long time, but that night, my answer satisfied him and I knew that little boy understood why we need to talk to our Heavenly Father everyday—because He loves us!

Chili and Chocolate Cake

Father God, thank you for loving Carson even more then I do. Thank you for showing yourself to him. And Lord Jesus, thank you for building up that little boy's faith in you. How wonderful it is to watch him seek you! You continually show yourself to him in such a way, that even at seven-years-old, he has no doubt in his mind that there is a God. I just recalled the day, a few years back, God, when Carson told me that it was hard to hear you because he couldn't see you, and now look what you are saying to him so that he can hear and in those words he can believe.

Father, I can never express what You mean to me and how You revealing Yourself to me on a daily basis, continues to show me more and more of who You really are! Thank you, Father.

I love you, Jesus.

                  In Your name I pray,

                          Amen

But Jesus said, "Let the little children come to Me, and do not forbid them; for of such is the kingdom of heaven."
                    Matthew 19:14 (NKJV)

Jesus said to him, "If you can believe, all things are possible to him who believes."
Mark 9:23 (NKJV)

So Jesus answered and said to them, "Have faith in God. For assuredly, I say to you, whoever says to this mountain, 'Be removed and be cast into the sea,' and does not doubt in his heart, but believes that those things he says will be done, he will have whatever he says. Therefore I say to you, whatever things you ask when you pray, believe that you receive them, and you will have them."
Mark 11:22–24 (NKJV)

Moving Forward

It seems like I should know you by now, you know so much about me.

It was a bit unsettling to sit down and put my life—my thoughts, my sins, my weaknesses, my trials, and my triumphs—on paper and then even more unsettling to think of sharing it with the world.

Therefore, I started to write this story very subtly. It was simply one victory at a time. I know, looking back on them, they may not seem like victories to you, but I can assure you, they were! They were victories, because I didn't give up!

As hard as it was some days to stay focused on Him, as much as I wanted to quit other days, I hung in there. Yes, granted some days I hung in there by the skin of my teeth, but I *hung*, nonetheless! Through it all, I never stopped listening to God. I will confess, many days his voice was a very distant whisper, and even more days the fog was so thick He was next to impossible to hear, but I never gave up.

And He certainly *never* gave up on me.

Even when I knew things weren't right, I was searching for answers, attempting to get myself back to where I needed to be. Yes, I took rabbit trails and granted, some of my rabbit trails took me off the track a lot longer than they should have, but my point is, I *never* stopped and said, "I quit."

You see, we play a starring role in our relationship with the Lord. Yes, He can lead us and guide us and direct our paths, but we *must* cooperate. We *must* allow Him to reign over us.

That is what free will is all about. We have the choice to accept the Lord and let Him work through us, or we have the choice to say, "Go away...I don't want you." I always *wanted* God, even during the time that I was mad at Him, and even when I wasn't sure if I could really trust Him, I never wanted to give up on Him.

Many times we have to reach a place of brokenness before God can use us. Being broken is not fun; it is usually a very painful process, but through our pain, we can become God's gain. When we reach that place where there is nothing left but God, well, at that point in our lives, God is *all we need!* That is the place where God can use us, right where we are.

Now, I know, in my heart of hearts, that I'm still not there yet. I doubt I ever will be in this life. But if you glean anything from my story, I pray that this is it:

Wherever you are, whatever is going on in your life, God wants to take you by the hand and walk with you through it. He wants to take care of you, and most of all, He loves you with a love that knows no boundaries!

He wants to be Your Savior, Your Lord, and Your Life. Go to Him now and receive His love!

When you are the neediest, He is the most sufficient.

When you are completely helpless, He is the most helpful.

When you feel totally dependent, He is absolutely dependable.

When you are the weakest, He is the most able.

When you are the most alone, He is intimately present.

When you feel you are the least, He is the greatest.

When you feel the most useless, He is preparing you.

When it is the darkest, He is the only Light you need.

When you feel the least secure, He is your Rock and Fortress.

When you are the most humble, He is most gracious.

When you can't, He can!
                              - Author Unknown

Now to Him who is able to do exceedingly abundantly above all that we ask or think, according to the power that works in us.
Ephesians 3:20 (NKJV)

Enough

After I wrote "Moving Forward," I thought I was finished with my story and with this book. In fact it was in the editing/proofreading stage and I was ready to get it published and move on, when God gave me a final chapter.

I really did think that all of my issues were finally out, but God showed me I still had one more hurdle to get past. It wasn't a new hurdle, just one I hadn't worked through completely. You know, God wants *all* of our sins, not just bits and pieces of them.

The wonderful thing about God's love is the sweetness that He can use to reveal something to us. God didn't beat me over the head with my Bible, while he was teaching me this new lesson. Instead, He very gently led me to and then through another healing process.

Not too long ago I began the process of what is so delicately referred to as, "the change of life." Now due to the fact that I'm a health nut and love my supplements, this process has been relatively painless thus far. I've not experienced many of the famous side effects: mood swings, hot flashes, etc..., but I have started having a very irregular menstrual cycle. For someone who has spent her life at a 28-day cycle, on the money, each and every month, that's been a bit of a challenge. Add to this the fact that I am only 44, I have small children, and I'm still not sure I'm ready to give up the idea of having another child and you can about picture my happiness for this newest development in the saga of my life.

This *change* can take several years or several months to work through, every person is different, but the ability to become pregnant/conceive is still very real, very possible—there are "change of life" babies everywhere.

Now, prior to this "change of life" stage I've been going through, I always knew the best time to conceive (as I mentioned to you earlier in my story) therefore, in order for me to prevent my chance of conceiving, I used to simply stay away from Bobby during those *danger* times. It obviously wasn't a foolproof method (as you can tell by my previous chapters), but if I stayed on top of my cycles, it at least gave me some sort of feeling of control over this issue. Hey, sometimes false control is better than no control. (Those of you who deal with issues of control will be able to relate to this statement.)

But now, with this new process going on, my body is changing that ability, and I no longer have any idea of when I might ovulate or when I might actually be able to conceive a child. And this is not really a very good place for me to be—I can hardly stand that constant feeling of never knowing what is going on with my body.

Despite the strain of this "change of life" stage, about six months into it, God's amazing grace enabled me to realize what had been going on with Bobby as well as enabled us to heal the wounds we had been nursing for far too long. For the first time in a long while we arrived at a place in our lives where we acted like newlyweds once again. We began to enjoy each other's company and we even started going out on dates again.

But this also caused me extreme stress, as I had no idea when the *danger* times were in my cycle. No idea of when my body might actually be in a time frame that I could become pregnant. I didn't know when I was in a *safe* time or when I was in a *danger* time.

So my body would start playing those tricks on me again. I would think it was about time for my period to start—I'd actually get the cramps and the headaches—but no period would come. And I'd start the worry process of "Am I pregnant?" "How can I go through with this again?" and thousands of other negative thoughts would fill my brain. But there would be no baby and two or three weeks later, the period would come and I'd feel like I'd received another reprieve.

The really rotten part of all of this for me was my divided mind. Part of me was afraid that I would get pregnant and part of me was afraid that I would never be pregnant again. I was torn in two. Half of me was scared to death to get pregnant and half of me was scared that I was finished in the baby making department, forever.

Remember, I had spent the last 18–20 years of my life wanting babies. It was so extremely difficult for me to just let that desire go. Through God's healing I was no longer standing in a pit of despair, spending each day agonizing over my lost babies and letting the desire for another baby overwhelm me, but I couldn't truthfully say to you that the desire was gone either. I would still find myself daydreaming about what it would be like if we had another little baby. How the boys would have fun with a new sibling, etc. I would replay these scenarios over again and again in my mind, on the occasions that I let myself go there. And I enjoyed these pictures. I truly didn't feel like I was ready to give that dream up.

I prayed and asked God to take this desire away. I told Him that if it wasn't from Him, I didn't want it. Although I wasn't letting the desire rule me, it was still there. It wasn't in the forefront of my mind, but it was definitely still floating about, if I was really honest with myself.

So what happened to bring my thoughts and desires into perspective? Well, one day one of my friends from church ended up in the hospital. She had been having stroke-like symptoms and, at age twenty, this was very disturbing. During the time she was in the hospital, her parents were out of town, so our church family rallied around her, giving her comfort and support. I headed down to the hospital myself to see her after dinner one night, and ended up sitting with her and another friend 'till late in the evening.

As I sat in that hospital room that evening, quietly chatting with the two of them, the night I lost baby Chance started to come back to me, in a very large, very unsettling way. I actually started talking about my time in the hospital when I had to deliver him, with the girls, thinking maybe if I just talked about the loss of the baby, the bad thoughts would leave my mind. But when I got home that night, I couldn't sleep. The grief and the pain were still heavy on my heart. The memories would not stop, as much as I prayed to release them.

Now, the good part was, I wasn't falling into the pit again, but I was definitely on the edge looking in, and I didn't like what I saw. I *did not* want to go there anymore.

The next morning, I got up and headed to my Friday bible study. We were working through Joanna Weaver's book, *Having A Mary Heart, In A Martha World.* That particular week we were working through the topic of *worry*. Now, I had actually extended this chapter another week, as there was so much great information in it and I have a very good friend, who I thought really needed this concept to sink in. She carried a lot of stress in her life and I was hoping that God would reveal to her something to help her through that teaching.

Myself, well, I felt like I had given up *worry* a while back, so I didn't really feel like there was anything in particular in the lesson for me, but I was very willing to stretch it out, if it would help my friend. Little did I know that the stretching out part was for me, but that is how the Lord works, so very subtly sometimes, not to knock us down, but to lift us up.

As I went through the scriptures, and started sharing a little bit about my previous night with my friends, I got this intense revelation that I had fallen under that very worry mode that I saw in my friend, which was really based on fear. The only difference was, she made her fear obvious to the group, whereas I had kept mine hidden within.

I had never really discussed this *fear* that I had been carrying—the fear I had of becoming pregnant, the fear that I might have to experience another painful loss. I had mentioned it once or twice, but I had never really shared those thoughts freely. My fear of pregnancy was an issue that I didn't want to discuss, because I wouldn't even admit to myself how nervous the thought of becoming pregnant made me, especially when I had not totally given up the idea of having another baby.

You can see the dilemma surrounding me. Scared to be pregnant, scared not to be pregnant. Not an easy place to be. Especially considering that I had no control over my cycles, no idea when I may or may not be able to conceive, never really sure if I might be pregnant or if I was just going through a longer cycle time.

God had continually been putting the thought *Trust Me* in my mind throughout the week, and I was continually answering Him, "I do." But that morning, I realized that I still carried fear in my heart. Fear of what would happen if I were to become pregnant again. And worry that I could *not* go through that experience again, that it would not be a time of joy for me, but rather another terrible burden that I would have to bear alone. I knew that such a thought process was not of God. A baby is a gift from God, the hope and promise of a new life for Him. But all that was in my mind regarding pregnancy was sorrow and fear.

I realized that I didn't trust God with this issue, because if I had, then if God were to give Bobby and I another child, I would be fine with it and would count the child as a blessing to us. I wanted another baby, but I truthfully did not believe that God would allow us to have another one. The pain and sorrow resulting from losing babies was so ingrained in my mind, that I had completely missed the concepts that God gives and that God can do all things and that if He were to give us another baby, it would be His gift and I would have to accept it and have faith in God's plan, not my own preconceived thoughts or ideas.

And on the flip side, I had to come to the realization that if another baby was not to be, then that was fine as well. Bobby and I were blessed with two very special little boys—our cup was running over. I had to recognize that we have a very special family, filled with love, just the way it is.

I left the Bible study that morning, with yet another piece of God revealed to me. He showed me that worry/fear can come in all sorts of packages, but they are all distractions from the enemy and something to keep us from drawing closer to Him. I went home and spent the afternoon simply resting in Him. The sweetness that came from His peace was so intense, yet so very calming. I didn't have to do anything. He was in control.

Later that evening, at church prayer time, His Spirit filled our gathering and it was during this time, that He showed me that *He was enough!*

If I have Jesus, I have enough! *He is enough!*

God's river of peace started flowing through me at that point and I realized that as long as I had Jesus, I truly would be okay.

There were so many verses to draw on with this thought, but I think the one that says it all is:

...Perfect love casteth out fear...
I John 4:18

Jesus is love. He is the perfection of love, and if He is in control, fear and worry must flee.
Thank you Father for your perfect love.
Amen

Joyce's Chili Recipe

1 package ground beef
1 package Mild Italian Sausage links
1 package McCormick's Chili Mix
1 yellow onion - chopped
2 large cans whole tomatoes
1 large can tomato sauce
1 large can kidney beans
2 small cans black beans
Chili Powder
Cayenne Pepper
Crushed Red Pepper
Cumin Powder

Remove the sausage from the sausage links and brown with ground beef in a Dutch oven. Add chopped onion.
Cook till brown.
Drain fat.
Crush whole tomatoes by hand and add to the meat mixture along with the tomato sauce and the beans.
Stir well.
Add the package of seasoning. Stir again, and then add your favorite seasonings to taste. Throw in a handful of sugar and let simmer for two hours, stirring occasionally.
Top with grated Mexican cheese.
Enjoy!

Notes

1. Max Lucado, *A Woman's Prayer for Everyday of the Year* (calendar) November 16, (Bloomington, MN: Garborg's, 2001)

2. Neva Coyle, *A Woman's Prayer for Everyday of the Year* (calendar) May 23, (Bloomington, MN: Garborg's, 2001)

3. Brenda Waggoner, *Fairy Tale Faith: Living in the Meantime When You Expected Happily Ever After*, p. 44, (Wheaton, IL: Tyndale House Publishers, Inc., 2003)

4. Janette Oke, *A Woman's Prayer for Everyday of the Year* (calendar) September 18, (Bloomington, MN: Garborg's, 2001)

5. Charles R. Swindoll, *A Woman's Prayer for Everyday of the Year* (calendar) January 6, (Bloomington, MN: Garborg's, 2001)

6. Waggoner, *Fairy Tale Faith*, p. 3.

7. Sheila Walsh, *Honestly*, p. 47, (Grand Rapids, MI: Zondervan, 1997)

8. Jeremy Camp, *Stay*, "I Still Believe," (Seattle, WA: BEC Recordings, 2002)

9. Waggoner, *Fairy Tale Faith*, p. 191.

10. Sheila Wash, *A Woman's Prayer for Everyday of the Year* (calendar) February 21, (Bloomington, MN: Garborg's, 2001)

11. Joanna Weaver, *Having A Mary Heart In A Martha World: Finding Intimacy With God in the Busyness of Life*, p. 195, (Colorado Springs, CO: Waterbrook Press, 2000)

12. Louis B. Wyly, *A Woman's Prayer for Everyday of the Year* (calendar) October 28, (Bloomington, MN: Garborg's, 2001)

13. Brenda Waggoner, *The Velveteen Woman: Becom-*

ing Real Through God's Transforming Love, p. 13, (Colorado Springs, CO: Chariot Victor Publishing, 1999)*

14. Waggoner, *The Velveteen Woman*, p. 11, 12

15. David Biebel, *If God Is So Good, Why Do I Hurt So Bad?* p. 138 (Westwood, NJ: Fleming H. Revell, Co., 1995)

16. Waggoner, *The Velveteen Woman*, p. 18, 19

17. Waggoner, *The Velveteen Woman*, p. 49

18. Waggoner, *The Velveteen Woman*, p. 39

19. Waggoner, *The Velveteen Woman*, p. 50

20. Judith Briles, *A Woman's Prayer for Everyday of the Year* (calendar) April 15, (Bloomington, MN: Garborg's, 2001)

21. Ralph Waldo Emerson, *A Woman's Prayer for Everyday of the Year* (calendar) March 16, (Bloomington, MN: Garborg's, 2001)

22. Dean Salyn, *All I Need*, "He Is Yahweh," (Canada: Vineyard Music, 2001)

23. Brenda Waggoner, *Fairy Tale Faith*, p. 156

---

*© 200- Cook Communications Ministries. The Velveteen Woman by Brenda Waggoner. Reprinted with permission. May not be further reproduced. All rights reserved.

The End...For Now

Writing this book has been such a special time for me. Lots of emotions flowing and being revisited but the end result is such peace. One day I was contemplating life and how we are here to encourage and lift each other up, and God gave me a really great illustration.

When we are in a swimming pool and drowning, we can't see the others who are drowning around us. We are too busy trying to save ourselves. We wouldn't even know if another drowned beside us. But once we climb up onto the raft or the lifeboat, we can then clearly see others in the pool who are also drowning. And it is our duty and desire to attempt to save them, but:

> * We can only save ourselves by reaching out, taking that required action.
> * We can only save someone else if they reach out to us and accept our assistance.
> * We have to be careful that we don't let the drowning people drag us back under.

My prayer in writing this story is that if you are drowning right now, that you please reach out and take that lifeline—it's worth the effort. If you are on the lifeboat, please reach out and help those drowning around you. God will bless you for your efforts, but be careful you don't get pulled back under yourself.

Thank you for allowing me to share my story of hope with you!

May God richly bless you!
Joyce

Not that I speak in regard to need, for I have learned in whatever state I am, to be content: I know how to be abased, and I know how to abound. Everywhere and in all things I have learned both to be full and to be hungry, both to abound and to suffer need. I can do all things through Christ who strengthens me.

Philippians 4:11–13, NKJV

Made in the USA
Columbia, SC
12 March 2018